REP RIPS REPS Weave

Projects, Instruction, and Inspiration

Lucienne Coifman

REP
RIPS
REPS Weave

Projects, Instruction, and Inspiration

Lucienne Coifman

HANDWOVEN ORIGINALS
NORTH HAVEN, CONNECTICUT
WWW.LUCIENNE-REPWEAVE.COM

To all of the weavers who will be using this book,
I wish you enjoyment and success.

© 2015 Lucienne Coifman

All rights reserved. No portion of this book may be reproduced by any means without written permission from the publisher, except for the purposes of review. The rep weave designs in this book are for personal use only and may not be produced for resale.

ISBN: 978-0-615-33674-9

Designer: Jeanne Criscola | Criscola Design
Editor: Deborah Cannarella
Technical Editor: Susan E. Horton
Draft Editors: Laurie Autio, Anne Graham, Janney Simpson
Photographers:
    Micah Beree: cover photo, pages 3, 16, 132, 139, 140, 153–162, 170, back cover
    Mara Lavitt: pages 61–67, 74, 77, 108–118, 124–131
    Robert Lisak: pages 28–59, 68–72, 78–107, 120, 122, 144, 150

Page 60: Table with inlaid water-hyacinth pattern, Fairhaven Furniture, New Haven, CT
Page 171: Portrait of author, Storytellers Photography

Acknowledgments

My friend and colleague, Betsey Haven, introduced me to rep weave. She used to weave placemats in two colors—mostly blue and off-white, in the traditional Colonial American style. At the time I was weaving clothing and fashion accessories, but I was inspired to try my hand at rep weaving that used more than two colors. *Et voila!* I was hooked.

After studying the technique of rep weaving for almost three decades, it felt right to start writing down my discoveries. At the request of my students, I decided to share my findings in a book.

I dedicate this book to my former students and to future novice weavers, who are still unknown to me and who I hope will be inspired by the projects I present here. I hope that these samplers and finished pieces will not only inspire them to learn more about rep weaving but will also challenge them and stimulate their creative juices!

Thank you to all of my fellow weavers who supported me during the many months—or shall I say years?—in which I've worked on this book. Without their help, feedback, and continued support, this book would not have been possible.

Laurie Autio	Luiz Cordeiro	Linda Edwards	Priscilla Racki
Donna Batsford	Fran Curran	Anne Graham	Janney Simpson

Thank you to all the students, teachers, and friends who encouraged me and helped me bring this book to life. Many of them read and reread the drafts under tough deadlines, but always with good humor.

Thank you to Janney Simpson for planting the initial seed for this book. Her constant inquiries about the project kept me going.

I am especially grateful to Susan Horton, a former student of mine, who is fluent with drafting programs and took on the task of setting up all of the drafts.

The photography was critical to showcasing the projects. I want to thank my photographers, Micah Beree, Robert Lisak, and Mara Lavitt, for doing such a superb job. A special thank-you to my son-in-law, Micah, who shot the cover photo and most of the photos in the gallery sections at the back of the book.

A special thank-you to my friend Susan Guagliumi, who allowed us to use her kitchen and living room for photo sessions. (Her screen porch was very much appreciated when there were several feet of snow outside and we had to photograph two beach chairs.) Thank you, too, to Fairhaven Furniture in New Haven, Connecticut, for allowing us to stage several photographs in their showrooms, and to Mara Lavitt for making those arrangements.

Thank you to my editor, Deborah Cannarella, whose superb organization and management of the timeline kept us on track. Her outstanding advice helped shape the material into a book.

My love and thanks to my daughters—Yael, Vanessa, and Karin—and to their families for being so patient. A special thank-you to my daughter Jessica, who spent many hours editing my first draft and helped shape the chapters. Finally, to my husband, Raphy, my Patron of the Arts, whose patience and understanding made this journey possible.

And, most important, a special thank-you to my new friend, Jeanne Criscola, whose easygoing attitude made the planning and designing of this book a true pleasure. Each meeting was uplifting and kept me focused and motivated. Jeanne, I am so fortunate to have crossed paths with you.

Contents

8 ABOUT REP WEAVE

9 *What Is Rep Weave?*
10 History
11 Equipment
12 About Warp Material
13 Determining the Warp Sett
13 About Weft Material

17 *Special Considerations for Rep Weavers*
19 Calculating Warp Length
22 Measuring Length
23 Finishing the Piece
24 How to Read the Drafts

28 TWO-SHAFT PROJECTS

29 *Only Two Shafts? No Problem!*
31 Breakfast Time *(table mat and placemats)*
35 Trellis *(table runner)*
39 Playing with Colors *(table runners)*
42 Turquoise and Sand *(bathroom rug)*

46 FOUR-SHAFT PROJECTS

47 *Two-Block Patterns on Four Shafts*
49 Windowpanes *(placemats and table runner)*
52 Rail Tracks *(kitchen rug)*
57 Noël *(table runner)*
61 Festival of Lights *(table runner)*
65 Color Changes *(placemats)*
69 Dinner for Two *(placemats and table runner)*

73 *Four-Block Patterns on Four Shafts*
75 Navajo Traditions *(sampler)*
79 Theme Variations *(placemats and table runner)*
83 Adding Colors *(table runner and placemats)*
87 Five Shades of Gray *(table mat)*

90 EIGHT-SHAFT PROJECTS

91 Four-Block Patterns on Eight Shafts
- 92 Waiting for Summer *(beach chair covers)*
- 97 Seven Shades of Red *(table runner)*
- 103 Undulations *(wall hanging)*
- 109 Double Steps *(rug)*

113 Eight-Block Patterns on Eight Shafts
- 115 Reflections *(wall hanging)*
- 121 Sitting Pretty *(bench cushion)*
- 125 Diamonds, Owl, Clown, and Butterfly *(table runner and mats)*

132 DESIGNING YOUR OWN PROJECTS

133 Planning a Rep Weave Pattern
- 134 About Color
- 135 The Six Basic Design Steps
- 136 Designing a Two-Block Project
- 140 Designing a Four-Block Project

144 LET'S PLAY

145 Game Boards and Mazes
- 146 Game Boards
- 151 Hop, Skip, and Jump Rug
- 152 *Tapu'at* Maze
- 153 Labyrinth of Color

154 THREE-DIMENSIONAL FORMS

155 Books, Bags, and Boxes
- 157 Book or iPad Cover
- 158 Two Bags
- 160 Three Little Boxes

- 163 *Appendix: More Drafting Styles*
- 169 *Yarn Sources*
- 169 *Recommended Books*
- 171 *About the Author*
- 172 *Index*

ABOUT REP WEAVE

What Is Rep Weave?

REP WEAVE is a weaving technique in which the warp threads are set very closely together to cover the weft threads completely. The weave structure is predominantly a warp-faced plain weave, and the finished fabric is ribbed. It is also reversible. The back is just the opposite of the front, so both faces are equally interesting and functional.

Unlike a warp-faced plain weave, which requires only one thickness of weft, rep weave uses two different thicknesses of weft. Its characteristic ribbed texture comes from the alternating heavy and fine wefts. Horizontal ribs corresponding to the heavy pick (multiple strands) of weft alternate with narrow lines, which correspond to the fine pick (single strand) of weft, which is the tie-down thread.

History

Rep weaving is a very old technique. Although historical information is difficult to find, fragments of rep weave fabrics have been found in South America, the Middle East, and North Africa. Bedouin tribes employed the technique, sewing long, narrow, rep weave bands together to make tents, bags, and other items. Central American Indians used rep weave as the foundation fabric for their clothing, on which they hand-embroidered colorful designs.

The method is now used all over the world. Surprisingly, in Sweden rep weaving is mainly associated with rugs, which are usually woven with only two or three colors. In the early 1980s, weavers in the United States began to discover rep weave through the many Scandinavian books on the subject. By the 1990s, rep weaving grew very popular, and weavers developed more colorful and complicated patterns.

REP, RIPS, REPP, REPS

In English, the technique of rep weaving is known as *rep* or *repp*. The word may be a corruption of the word "rib," which is a characteristic of the fabric. In French, the method is called *reps*—another possible source of the English term. In Sweden, the technique is called *rips*.

The Swedish word *ripsmatta* is sometimes mistakenly used to refer to rep weaving. *Ripsmatta* is not a technique—the word simply means "a rug or mat that has been made with rep weave."

Equipment

I prefer to weave on a Jack-type loom with a heavy beater, but I have used many kinds of looms for rep weaving, including table looms (for narrower pieces). I work on an eight-shaft loom, which allows for more design possibilities, but you can also create rep weave designs working with only two shafts (see pages 28–45).

I rarely weave with wool, but if you'd like to, you will need a very heavy loom—perhaps a countermarch equipped with a weighted beater. You'll also need tight, fine-grade, two- or three-ply wool, which is easier to work with than other weights. Keep in mind that rep weave requires a lot of heddles to accommodate the many warp threads. You need to plan ahead of time to be sure you have enough heddles for each project.

When weaving, I work with stick shuttles that are as wide as the piece. I use the sharp edge of the stick shuttle like a sword, both to clear the shed and to pass the weft. If my piece is very wide, I use a boat shuttle for the fine weft and a ski shuttle for the heavy weft. I find a long sword useful for clearing the shed when necessary.

OPPOSITES, CONTRASTS, AND PAIRS

Rep weave is a weave structure made up of opposites and contrasts. The two layers of the fabric, made up of heavy and fine threads, interlace. The top layer is usually dark and the bottom layer is a contrasting color. When thinking about rep weave, think in terms of opposites, of positive and negative:

   Top layer–Bottom layer
   Background–Pattern
   Heavy weft–Fine weft
   Dark–Light

Or you can think of rep weave in terms of pairs:

   2 shafts (per block design)
   2 treadles (one for the pattern weft, one
      for the fine tie-down thread weft)
   2 wefts (heavy and fine)

About Warp Material

You can use many different types of materials for a rep weave warp as long as they are strong and can sustain very tight tension. Cotton is my warp yarn of choice because it's so versatile. Wool, linen, Cottolin, and some of the new fibers—such as Tencel—are also suitable for certain projects.

Yarn weights are indicated by two numbers, separated by a slash. The first number refers to the thickness of the thread—the higher the number, the finer the thread. The second number indicates the number of plies in the thread.

My favorite warp material is 5/2 mercerized cotton. Its beautiful sheen and wide color palette make it the perfect-weight thread for table linens, accessories, and wall hangings. I prefer 3/2 mercerized cotton for rugs and large wall hangings. An 8/4 carpet warp is extremely versatile. It's strong and offers a wide color spectrum. I mostly use it for table mats and rugs. A double thread of 5/2 mercerized cotton is perfect for rugs, giving them some extra weight (see "Double Steps," page 109).

For finer pieces—such as towels, lightweight scarves, bags, and boxes—I sometimes use 8/2 unmercerized cotton. Tencel is also a good choice and will produce a more luxurious result. Finer warp threads are sometimes treated as double threads to form one "working end"—a technique you'll find in many Swedish rep weaving books. A double thread of fine 10/2 mercerized cotton, as in the project "Five Shades of Gray" (see page 87), will improve the weft coverage.

CHOOSING WARP YARNS

I have indicated the materials you'll need for each of the projects in this book—but if you would like to make substitutions or would eventually like to create your own designs, here are some rules of thumb. You'll need to keep the warp sett in mind, too (see facing page).

When choosing warp yarns, consider what type of piece you are making to be sure the materials are durable enough for the finished weaving's intended use.

Wall hangings: 3/2, 5/2 mercerized cotton

Rugs: 8/4 carpet warp, 3/2 or 5/2 double threads

Table mats: 5/2, 10/2 mercerized cotton, 22/2 Cottolin

Towels, scarves, accessories: 8/2 unmercerized cotton or 10/2 mercerized cotton, Tencel

Determining the Warp Sett

Sett is the number of ends per inch (epi) in the warp. In rep weaving, there are two options for the sett of the warp. Traditionally the warp has a **tight sett**, which means the warp will completely cover the weft. Most of the projects in this book require a tight sett.

When the warp has a **loose sett**, the weft peeks through and slightly changes the overall color of the piece (see "Color Changes," page 65). A loose sett is best when you want to emphasize the weft threads to create a certain visual effect (as when using rag strips as your weft, for example).

After you have chosen the warp material, the next important step is to establish the correct sett for that particular yarn. To determine the sett, wrap the warp thread as closely as possible around a ruler for a length of 1 in. to determine the epi. Then multiply the number of wrapped threads by 2 or 2½, depending on the density of the weave structure and the desired weight of the finished fabric. For example, I would use a sett of 2½ when making a rug or wall hanging.

> **Warp Sett** = *[number of wrapped threads per 1 in.] x [2 or 2½, depending on project]*

RECOMMENDED WARP SETTS

The sett of the warp threads, which determines the density of the warp, is measured in ends per inch, or epi. (In the chart below, there is no loose sett indicated for doubled fine threads. Doubled fine threads act as a single end, and with a loose sett, the warp ends would not cover the weft.)

	Tight	*Loose*
8/4 carpet warp	30–32 epi	24 epi
16/2 mercerized cotton *(doubled)*	48 epi	—
10/2 mercerized cotton	60 epi	48 epi
10/2 mercerized cotton *(doubled)*	40 epi	—
5/2 mercerized cotton	40-48 epi	32 epi
3/2 mercerized cotton	32 epi	24 epi
8/2 unmercerized cotton	48 epi	40 epi
8/2 Tencel	48 epi	40 epi
22/2 Cottolin	48 epi	40 epi

About Weft Material

Rep weave is characterized by the use of two different weights of weft threads: **heavy and fine**. The weft is completely covered by the dense warp threads and only peeks out at the selvedges. So, for the heavy weft, it's nice to choose colors that match the colors of the warp. The color of the fine weft is not as important as you will only see a dot of it at the selvedge ends.

Luckily, there are several suppliers of "string yarn" of different thicknesses suitable for weft material—string yarn is durable

and doesn't fuzz with handling and washing. It is easy to find and is available in many colors and weights. You can make your weft simply by wrapping several threads around the shuttle to the desired thickness. You can also make heavy weft from mop cotton, cotton rope, multistrand cotton, and strips of rags.

I have gotten into the habit of making my own weft because it allows me to get the exact color and thickness I want. You can make your own weft easily by using your ball winder and a few cones of yarn. First gather as many cones or tubes of the shades of yarn that you have decided to use (you could work with all the colors in the warp or just some of them). Using the ball winder, make a substantial-size ball with, let's say, four threads. Take the ball off the winder and add four more threads from your cones to the ball, so you now have a ball with eight threads. Continue adding to the ball until you have the correct number of ends for the warp sett of your yarn (see page 13). This technique is not only a very efficient way to make your weft, it also reduces fiber waste.

The fine weft (which is the binding weft) can be the same material as the warp or somewhat finer—but it must be strong. The greater the difference in weight between the two weft materials, the sharper the ribs will appear in the finished piece. The color blending will also be less pronounced. Most often I use 10/2 mercerized cotton for the fine weft. For more delicate pieces I use 20/2 mercerized cotton.

Weft thickness is of great importance in rep weaving. It is best to weave a sample of your project before you begin to be sure that the finished piece will have the right proportions (height to width). The shape of the woven designs must be perfectly symmetrical and square (or slightly elongated if you are measuring them under tension).

WEFT SETT

Keeping the weft sett consistent as you weave is important in maintaining the shape of the woven designs. To determine the weft sett, I count the number of ribs (heavy and fine) in 2 in. of the length of the woven fabric:

Weft Sett = *[the number of ribs in 2 in. of woven fabric]*

Special Considerations for Rep Weavers

THERE ARE MANY BOOKS AND WEBSITES for beginner weavers that cover in detail the basic processes of winding the warp, setting up the loom, and weaving. If you are a beginner weaver or wish to review the processes step by step, you may want to consult one of those sources before you begin your project. In this book, I am providing a list of guidelines specific to rep weaving for you to keep in mind as you weave. It took me much trial-and-error before I felt comfortable and had developed a good level of skill with rep weaving. I've gathered here some of the important key points I learned along the way.

The goal of this book is to provide step-by-step information about rep weaving. There are projects for beginning weavers and some for more advanced ones. The patterns are presented in order of complexity.

Calculating Warp Length

Always be generous when making your warp. There is nothing more upsetting than being able to weave only three-and-a-half placemats!

When calculating the length of the warp, take into consideration the thickness of the weft. The weaving will contract more when using a heavy weft than it will when using a finer one. There is also more take-up when using a heavy warp thread such as 3/2 mercerized cotton than there will be when using 10/2 mercerized cotton. On the other hand, there is relatively no draw-in along the width of warp. The heavy weft compensates for the slight narrowing of the piece in the weaving.

In general I estimate 20 to 30 percent of total warp length for take-up: 10 to 12½ percent shrinkage (if the piece will be washed) plus 10 to 18 percent contraction in the warp. While weaving, to maintain the design, you need to elongate square blocks (as in "Traditional Checkerboard," page 146) to account for tension and shrinkage. Add about 10 percent to the block length. The exact amount is based on your woven sample. You need to add enough length to weave complete ribs.

Adding extra warp length is always a good idea. It's also a good idea to make samples with different weft thicknesses. Keep good records of the weft samplers, counting the number of ribs to determine each weft sett. Also measure the length of the weaving with a tape measure (see page 22).

MAKING THE WARP

When making the warp, use two warp threads together (one from the top layer and one from the bottom layer, which are usually two different colors). Separate the threads with your fingers as you wind the warp. Secure the warp with many ties (chokers), remembering to secure the cross, too

SAMPLE CALCULATION OF THE WARP LENGTH FOR A RUG

Finished length 36 in.	36 in.
Hems, 2 x 4 in.	8 in.
Laundry shrinkage, 10% of finished length	4 in.
Take-up of 18–25% of finished length	8 in.
	56 in. woven from hem to hem
	+ 36 in. loom waste
	92 in. total warp length

Tips for Loom Setup and Weaving

Sleying

- When dressing the loom from front to back, as I do, begin with sleying.
- In rep weaving, the warp is multisleyed to create a dense fabric. Always handle the thread pairs together.
- Keep checking your warp color sequence (see page 25) as you progress.

Threading

- Before starting to thread, count the heddles.
- Always grab together the two or four threads in the same dent—to eliminate crosses between dents.
- Thread small groups at a time, checking your work often.
- Tie the small repeats before starting a new one.
- There is no reason to add extra thread for a floating selvedge. The correct rotation of the shuttles will lock the selvedge ends (as explained on the facing page).

Winding the Warp

- Beam on tightly—the warp has many ends to the inch.
- As you wind onto the beam, pack the warp with brown paper, cardboard, or wooden sticks to create tension.
- Maintain the width of the warp on the back bar by tying on some heavy threads or Velcro ties to guide the warp. You could also use a raddle to guide the warp.
- Tie the warp onto the front beam in small groupings of no more than ½ in. of warp yarns. Trim the ends.

Tying Up the Treadles

- With a four-shaft loom, use a direct tie-up, so the shafts can be raised independently.
- If you wish to tie up by block, remember each heavy-weft treadle has a counterpart—the fine-weft treadle. Tie up the treadles in the opposite way to produce a tabby weave.
- The pairs of treadles needed to weave a block are most often next to each other.

- With an eight-shaft loom, if you are using a traditional tie-up, you sometimes have to re-tie, because you need more combinations than you have available treadles. In this case, use a skeleton tie-up that allows all sixteen combinations (see page 101). By pressing two treadles, you can open the shed more easily. (A few of the eight-shaft projects in this book provide drafts for both regular and skeleton tie-ups.)

Weaving

Several rules apply strictly to weaving rep weave. They ensure the proper handling of the two wefts and are important to the overall look of the finished fabric.

- Both wefts must lie straight in the shed—no arching or the fabric will buckle.
- Pass the shuttles in the same direction and sequence: heavy weft first, followed by the fine weft.
- **To maintain good selvedges, the heavy and fine wefts must interlace.** Pay attention to the point where the fine weft exits. If the fine weft thread is under the last warp thread, place the shuttle on top of your weaving. If the fine weft thread is over the last warp thread, pass the shuttle under the heavy weft and then place it on top of your weaving. The interlacing threads firmly lock the selvedges.
- Always give a good twist to the heavy weft at the turn—you'll have a better-rounded selvedge.
- Before weaving the fine weft, give it a firm tug at the selvedge end. You will notice that the turn of the heavy weft forms more of a curve.
- When starting the heavy weft, splice the thread, cutting 2 in. of one half. Grab 1 in. of the hanging tail and give it a good twist. Insert the tail into the shed, making it a full weft thickness. Leave just a little bit of the bend extending. Inserting the fine weft in the twist will help position the turn correctly. Passing the next fine weft will secure the heavy weft thread. To end the last heavy pick, taper it and turn it back into the same shed.
- When adding a heavy weft thread, splice the old and the new weft threads in several places and overlap them in the same shed.
- Sometimes, when changing the blocks, the last fine weft of the old block will be in the same shed as the heavy weft of the new block. No problem—the overlap will not show in the finished weaving and it will allow you to maintain the correct rotation of the shuttles.

Measuring Length

Keeping the weaving at a perfect length is difficult in rep weave. Watch your beat! Your beat pressure may vary, which is not easy to notice at first, and the tension of your warp may gradually change as you advance your warp. Check and maintain your weft sett. (It's okay to have some slight variations in length, however, even on matching pieces—placemats of different lengths will still look just fine on the table.)

I use two different methods to measure my pieces. The first method is to run a measuring tape along the fabric and carefully record the length as I go along (always measuring the piece under tension). The other method is to count the ribs as the design progresses. It is essential that you record both measurements carefully. They will keep you on track.

Rep weave demands that the warp is in high tension at all times. It is important to maintain that tension even when you're done weaving for the day. Relaxing the warp can alter the measurements.

Because of the high tension, you need to pay close attention to the height of the blocks in the rep weave design. Always extend the height of the blocks either by adding an extra rib or by increasing the number of ends in the heavy weft. When the fabric is off the loom, the warp will relax, and the block will be perfectly square.

THREE IMPORTANT WEAVING MEASUREMENTS

Woven length = length of the piece while on the loom, under tension

Raw length = length of the piece when off the loom

Finished length = length of the piece after washing and hemming

Finishing the Piece

When taking the piece off the loom, be sure to check for errors or missed threads. You can correct them easily with a needle and thread. Sometimes you'll find that the fine weft is not binding, either between the two pattern wefts or at the selvedge if the two weft threads did not interlace correctly.

To wash or not to wash? To avoid shrinkage, I don't wash rugs, wall hangings, or any woolen pieces—but you should wash all table pieces to allow for shrinking. I usually wash the pieces in the sink with a little dishwashing liquid. I then dry the pieces flat. Never put the piece in a clothes dryer—the process of machine-drying will deform the shape and pattern of the weaving, and the friction will weaken the fiber and fuzz the piece.

Most of the projects in this book are finished with a simple hem. Be sure to use the fine weft at the hem end so the fabric edge won't be too bulky to triple-fold. The fine weft may tend to narrow the piece but it's not a problem in the hem.

Although loose fringe at the ends of the piece may look nice when the fabric is just off the loom, fringe tends to fray with repeated washings. If you do wish to finish with fringes, I recommend twisting or braiding the ends. The effect is especially nice on a heavy rug or wall hanging. Because the warp is so dense, overhand knots on fringed ends will not lie flat.

How to Read the Drafts

This section will help you understand how to read the rep weaving drafts I use for the projects throughout this book. The chapter, "Planning a Rep Weave Pattern" (page 133) will explain how to think through the process if you would like to draft your own rep weave designs. The appendix on page 163 provides examples of the Scandinavian style of drafting rep weave patterns.

Profile Draft

Rep weave is a block weave. For almost every project in this book I have provided a profile draft—which is a type of shorthand for indicating the sequence of blocks in the pattern. The profile draft also indicates the number of warp threads in each unit (profile square) of the block.

The profile drafts in this book follow these basic rules for indicating the block weave patterns:

1. Each block is designated by a capital letter (A, B, C, D, E, F, G, H).
2. Each block is threaded on two shafts that are next to each other. Each shaft is threaded with a contrasting color—one for the top layer (background) and one for the bottom layer (pattern), unless the design has a solid line (see "Rail Tracks," page 52, and "Noël," page 57).
3. The width of a block is determined by the number of warp ends the block contains. You establish the width of the columns or blocks when threading.

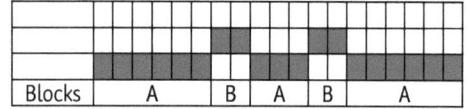

In the rep weave pattern shown in the profile draft at left, there are two blocks (A, B). The number of squares in each block of the profile draft varies according to the width of the block. This profile draft is for the coaster shown in the photo on page 27.

Warp Color Sequence *(color key)*

The warp color sequence shows the color sequence of the warp. You will follow this color sequence as you wind the warp onto the warping board: two blue ends together 6 times, one blue and one white end together 102 times, and two blue together 6 times. The sample coaster has only two colors: blue and white. There are 126 blue threads and 102 white threads in each of the two blocks. All of the white threads and some of the blue threads are in the bottom layer (unshaded).

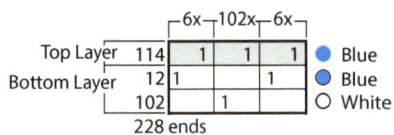

Threading Key

Each block has a specific threading key, which establishes the threading draft. The number of warp ends will vary according to the width of the block. This two-block pattern is woven on four shafts. The top layer of each block (which forms the background) is indicated with shading. The bottom layer of each block (which forms the pattern) is unshaded.

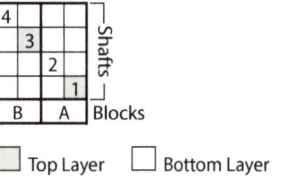

Threading Draft

The threading draft indicates the order in which the warp ends are threaded through the heddles. The draft is read from right to left, horizontally, with one row for each shaft. The draft also indicates the sequence of color ends per block.

The sample coaster has a thin solid-blue border—which means both layers of the border are blue. The border is threaded as an A block. You can thread solid lines in any block, but I usually use two adjacent shafts. Sometimes it is easiest to use the shafts that hold the fewest number of threads.

Some of the projects have long threading drafts and show only half of the draft with the center point of the design marked C (see page 76, for example). To complete the pattern, you would reverse threading (from B to A), continuing to alternate shafts, beginning with the top layer.

ABOUT REP WEAVE

Tie-Up

The tie-up indicates which shafts are tied to which treadles. The vertical columns indicate the shaft tie-up for each of the four treadles and for each of the two blocks.

Treadling Draft *(treadling sequence)*

The treadling draft determines the order in which you use the pair of treadles to create the pattern. Each row of the treadling draft corresponds to a rib of the fabric (made up of a heavy weft and a fine weft). Note the draft symbols for the alternating heavy and fine weft threads.

- Fine weft
- Heavy weft

When the treadling draft is long, only half of the draft is shown, with the center point of the design marked C (see page 40, for example). To complete the pattern, reverse the treadling sequence, keeping the heavy weft first, followed by the fine weft.

For each of the projects in this book, you'll find a close-up photograph of the fabric that shows the ribs that correspond to the treadling draft.

The Project Drafts

I have provided all the essential information needed to weave each of the projects in this book. The threading draft is drawn horizontally. The treadling draft is vertical. The tie-up draft is at the top of the treadling sequence.

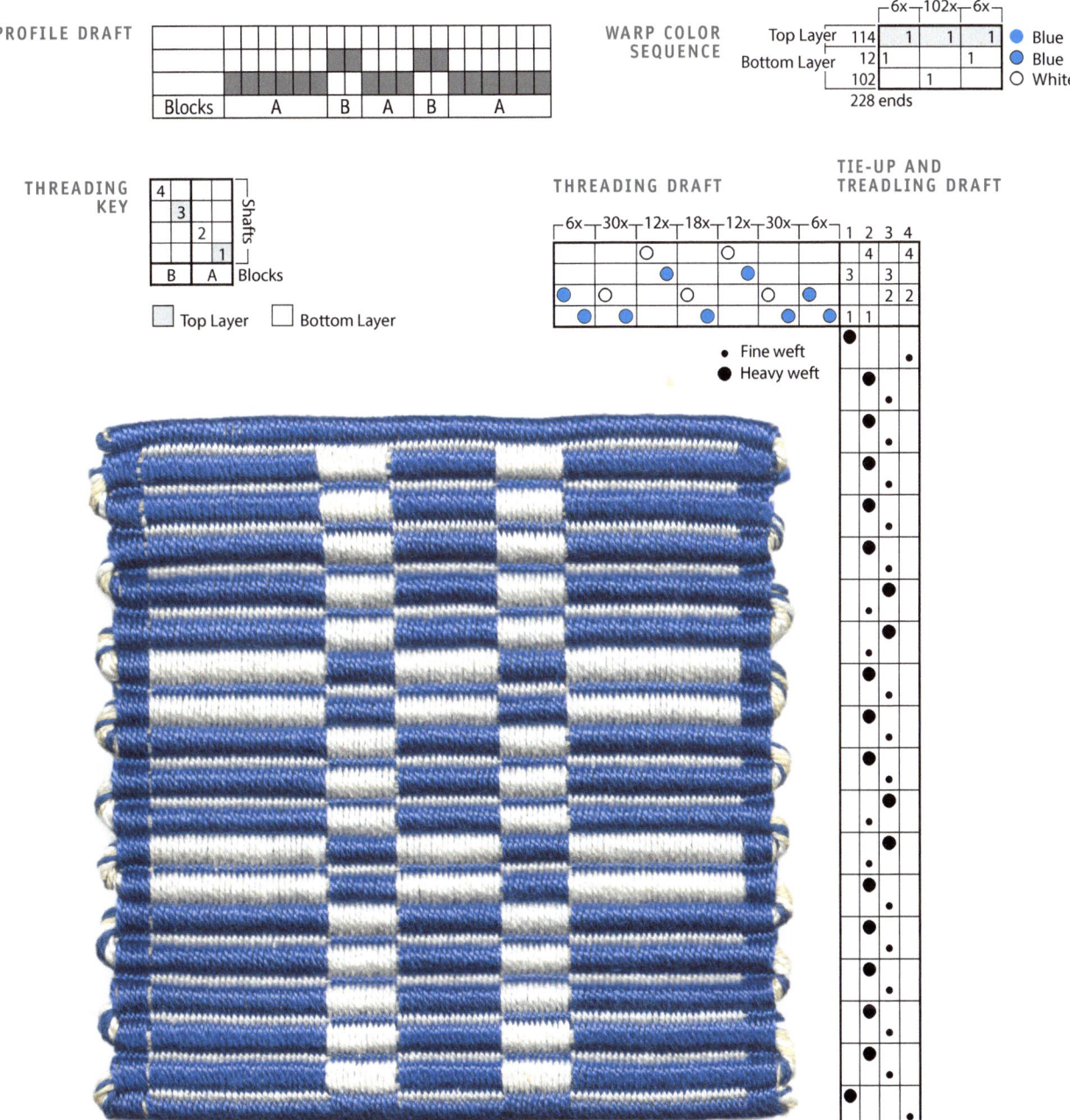

Only Two Shafts? No Problem!

REP WEAVE DESIGNS do not need to be complex. Most often, less is more. You can weave any simple two-block design with only two shafts. When working with two shafts, the weaving of one block affects the other.

There are four projects in this chapter, all designed for two shafts, but if your loom has four and you want to use them, by all means do (see page 40).

"Breakfast Time" (page 31), is a set of two placemats and a table mat, perfect for setting the breakfast table. The warp is 3/2 mercerized cotton in three colors. The heavy cotton has fewer ends per inch, so you will be working with a reasonable number of threads.

The "Trellis" table runner (page 35) is woven in 5/2 mercerized cotton in four colors. The design is a traditional windowpane pattern. One side has more colors than the other, but both sides are interesting.

The "Playing with Colors" table runners (page 39) are another simple rep weave design made with many colors. The same color appears on the top layer (threaded on shaft 1) and later on the bottom layer (threaded on the opposite shaft).

"Turquoise and Sand" (page 42), introduces two weave structures: épinglé and bengaline. Épinglé, which uses two different thicknesses of weft material, is the traditional rep weave structure. Bengaline is a warp-faced weave that uses only a heavy weft. You can weave this small rug on any type of floor loom. I wove it on an upright tapestry loom. The process was quite pleasant because the beater was heavy and gave a tight beat. I had so much fun with this rug I decided to weave another one, to put in front of the fireplace. I added a small pillow, too.

TABLE MAT AND PLACEMATS

Breakfast Time

These two matching placemats and accent table mat make an inviting setting for the breakfast table. The reverse side of the fabric is the opposite pattern of the first, so each piece is reversible.

MATERIALS

Finished dimensions: table mat 12 in. x 18 in.; placemats 12 in. x 17 in.

Warp	3/2 mercerized cotton (WEBS): Alabaster, Madder Brown, Amber Gold
Weft	
fine	10/2 mercerized cotton (WEBS), Alabaster
heavy	8 threads of 3/2 mercerized cotton (WEBS): 4 threads Alabaster, 2 threads Madder Brown, 2 threads Amber Gold
Sett	32 epi.
Reed	8 dents per inch
Sley	4 ends per dent; thread 1 end per heddle
Total ends	384
Width in reed	12 in.
Warp length	3 yd. *(loom waste included)*
Weft sett	7 ribs (heavy and fine) per 2 in.
Length on loom	table mat 23 in.; placemats 22 in. *(under tension, hems included)*
Length off loom	table mat 21.5 in.; placemats 20.75 in.
Finished length	table mat 18.5 in.; placemats 17 in. *(washed, hemmed)*

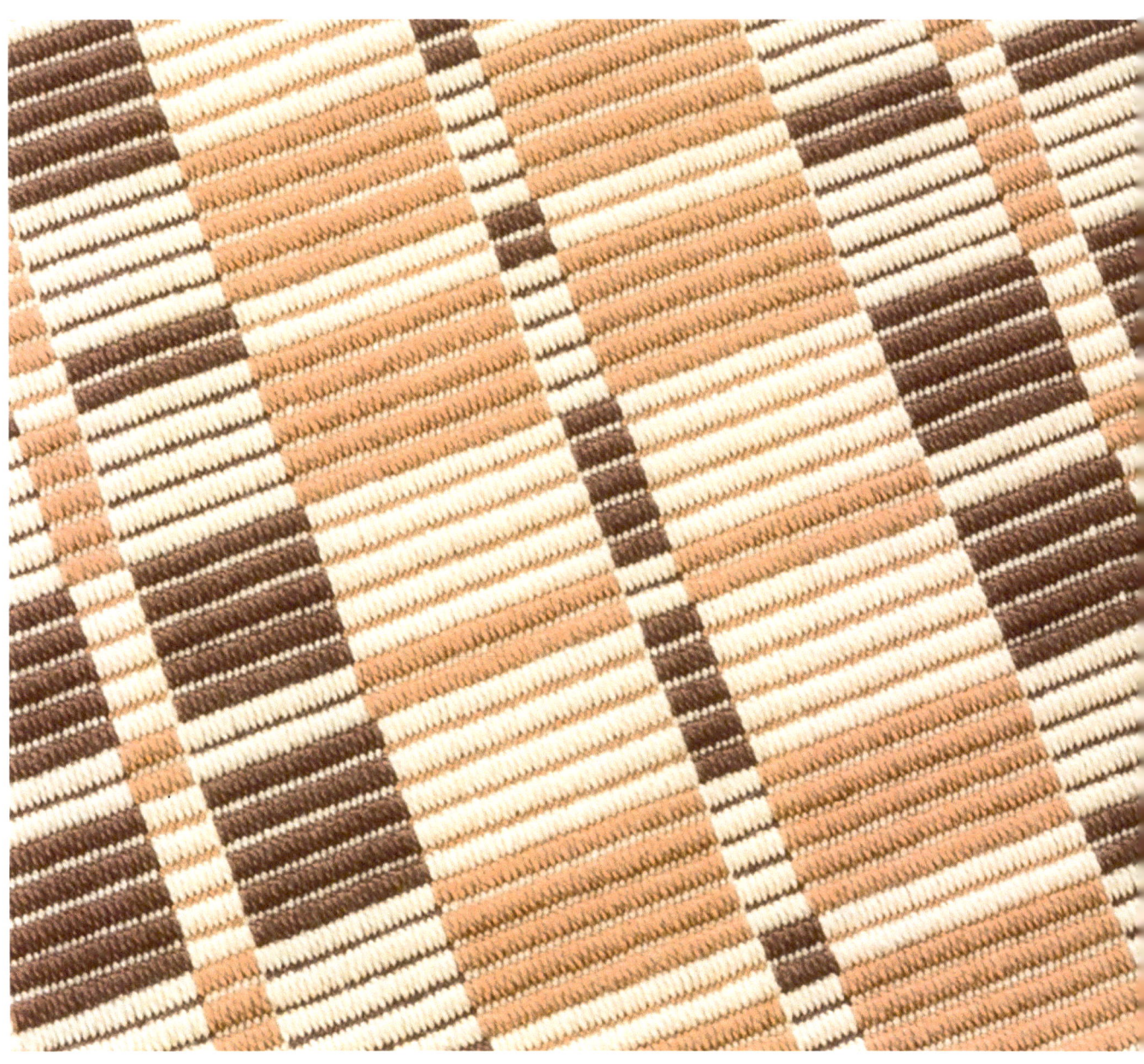

The 3/2 mercerized cotton warp shrank more than I expected but the placemats were still a generous size on the table. Remember that when using a heavy warp, you can expect a larger contraction of the ribs than with a fine warp—and therefore a larger take-up of the warp length.

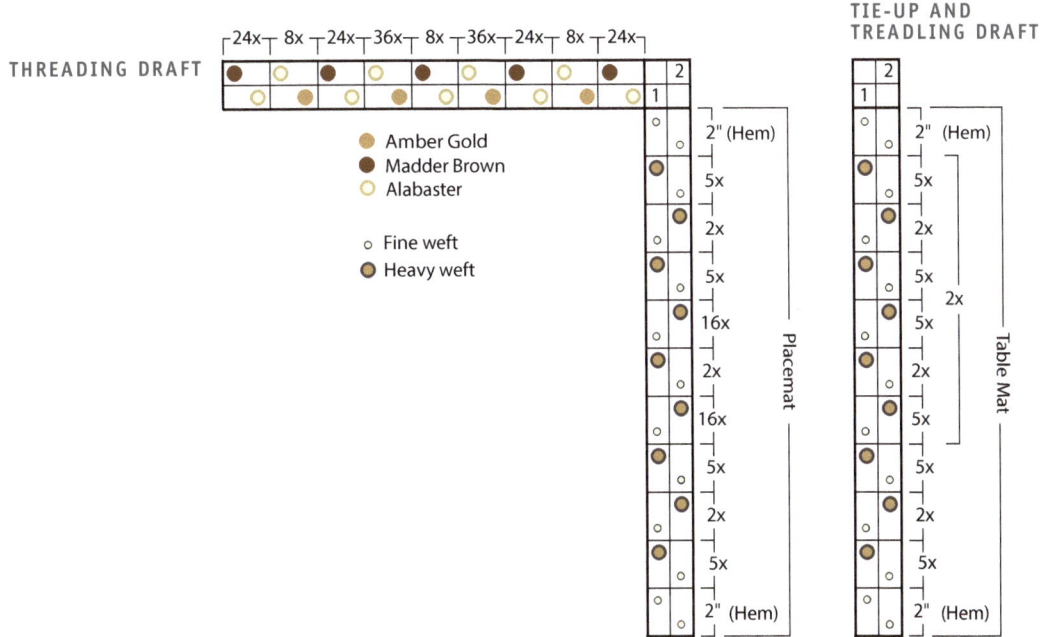

WEAVING

Start by weaving a hem with only the fine weft for 2 in., alternating shafts 1 and 2. Be sure not to arch the weft, or you'll get a wavy hem.

Follow the treadling sequence using both wefts. Keep the shuttles going in the same direction to maintain good selvedges (see page 21). When changing treadling, the new heavy weft shot will be in the same shed as the previous fine weft shot—this won't detract from the weaving and will help keep the shuttle rotation in the correct order. End the weaving with a hem.

TABLE RUNNER

Trellis

This colorful runner is woven in a traditional windowpane pattern. One side of the weaving has more colors than the other, but both sides are interesting and attractive.

MATERIALS

Finished dimensions: 12 in. x 43 in.

Warp	5/2 mercerized cotton (UKI): Deep Purple, Royal, Copen, Magenta
Weft	
fine	10/2 mercerized cotton (UKI), Black
heavy	12 threads of 5/2 mercerized cotton (UKI), Deep Purple
Sett	40 epi
Reed	10 dents per inch
Sley	4 ends per dent; thread 1 end per heddle
Total ends	480
Width in reed	12 in.
Warp length	2.5 yd. *(loom waste included; allows plenty of length for sampling, too)*
Weft sett	8 ribs (heavy and fine) per 2 in.
Length on loom	49 in. *(under tension, hems included)*
Length off loom	47 in.
Finished length	43 in. *(washed, hemmed)*

WARP COLOR SEQUENCE

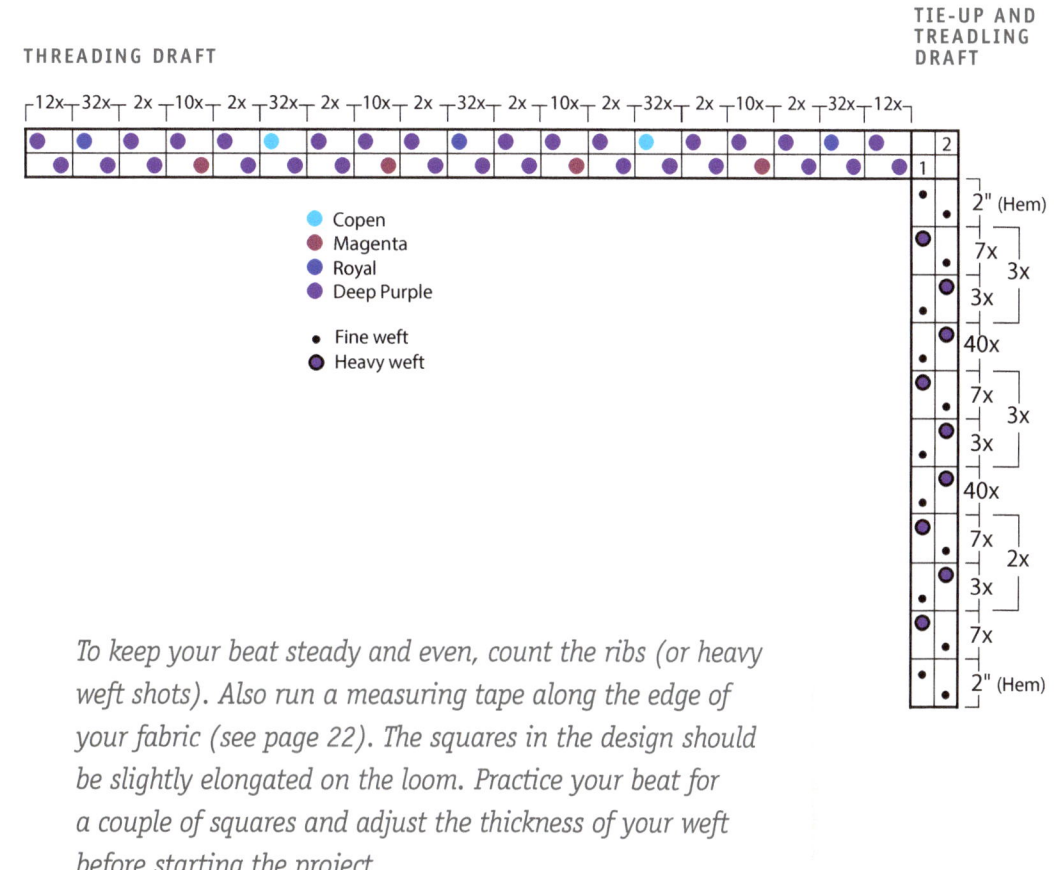

	24x	32x	4x	10x	4x	32x	4x	10x	4x	32x	4x	10x	4x	32x	4x	10x	4x	32x	24x	
64						1								1						● Copen #18
40				1				1				1				1				● Magenta #102
96		1								1								1		● Royal #16
280	1		1		1		1		1		1		1		1		1		1	● Deep Purple #120

480 ends

THREADING DRAFT

TIE-UP AND TREADLING DRAFT

- ● Copen
- ● Magenta
- ● Royal
- ● Deep Purple

- • Fine weft
- ⬤ Heavy weft

To keep your beat steady and even, count the ribs (or heavy weft shots). Also run a measuring tape along the edge of your fabric (see page 22). The squares in the design should be slightly elongated on the loom. Practice your beat for a couple of squares and adjust the thickness of your weft before starting the project.

WEAVING

Start by weaving a hem with only the fine weft for about 2 in., alternating shafts 1 and 2. Be sure not to arch the weft, or you'll get a wavy hem.

Follow the treadling sequence using both wefts, keeping the shuttles moving in the same direction.

TABLE RUNNERS

Playing with Colors

Here's an opportunity to play with color! This table runner design is colorful on both the front and back because of the varied colors of the warp threads. There is a different treadling sequence for each runner. It's easy to make your own variation—and I encourage you to do so! The long runner shown here is Runner #2 in the draft.

MATERIALS

Finished dimensions: short table runner 13 in. x 27 in.; long table runner 13 in. x 48 in.

Warp	5/2 mercerized cotton (UKI): Wine, Deep Turq, Maroon, Champagne, Medium Brown, Duck, Deep Purple, Deep Beige, Quarry
Weft	
fine	10/2 mercerized cotton (UKI), Black
heavy	12 threads of 5/2 mercerized cotton (UKI): 6 threads Medium Brown, 6 threads Maroon
Sett	40 epi
Reed	10 dents per inch
Sley	4 ends per dent, thread 1 end per heddle
Total ends	512
Width in reed	12.8 in.
Warp length	2.75 yd. for two runners *(loom waste included)*
Weft sett	8 ribs (heavy and fine) per 2 in.
Length on loom	short runner 31 in.; long runner 54 in. *(under tension, hems included)*
Length off loom	short runner 30 in.; long runner 52 in.
Finished length	short runner 27 in.; long runner 48 in. *(washed, hemmed)*

TWO-SHAFT PROJECTS

WARP COLOR SEQUENCE

TIE-UP AND TREADLING DRAFT

THREADING DRAFT

Runner #2
Treadle A to C then B to A, keeping the weft pairs in the correct order: heavy weft first, then fine weft.

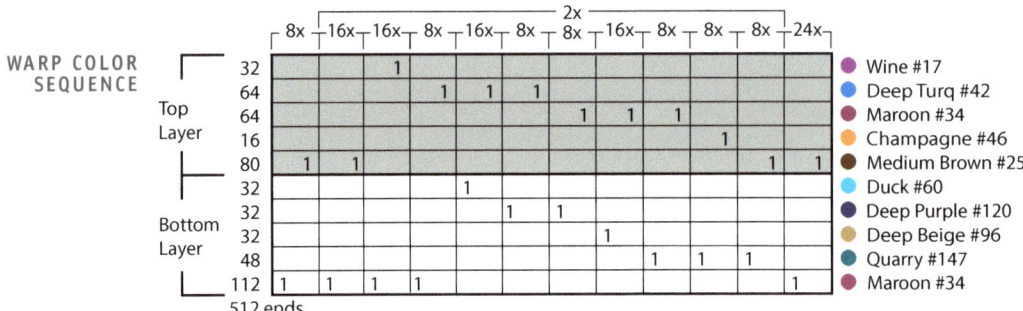

TIE-UP FOR FOUR SHAFTS

To weave these two runners requires a lot of threads and a lot of heddles. Spreading them over four shafts rather than two will make it easier to weave and to treadle. When you are working with four shafts, two shafts do the work of one.

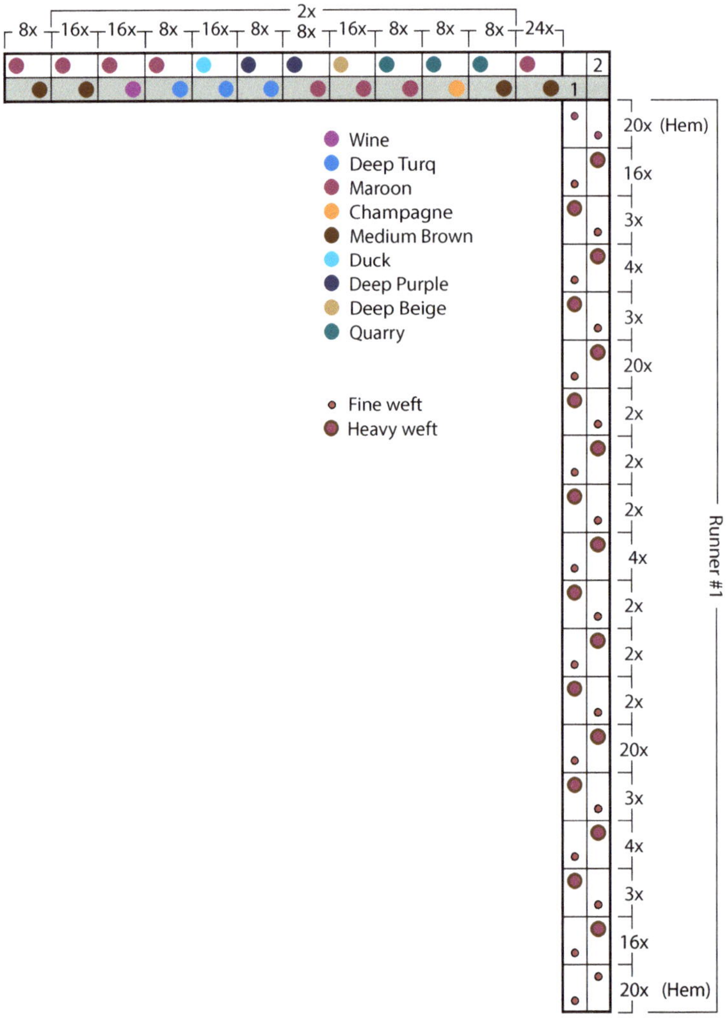

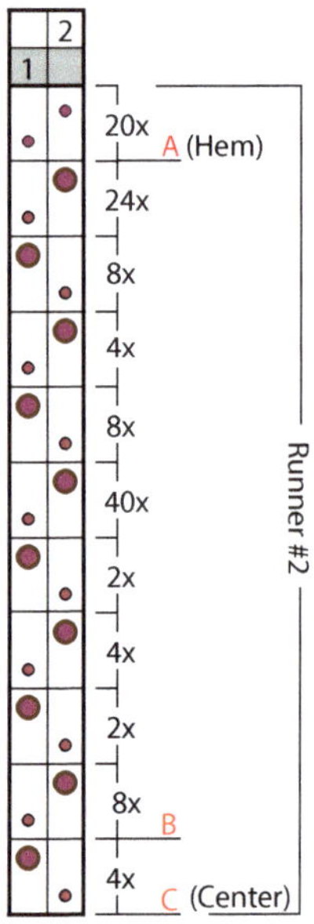

Shafts 1 and 3 (heavy weft) Shafts 2 and 4 (fine weft)
Shafts 2 and 4 (heavy weft) Shafts 1 and 3 (fine weft)

WEAVING

Start by weaving a hem with only the fine weft. Follow either treadling sequence, using both shuttles and working them in the same direction. Remember: whenever you switch to another block and change treadling, the heavy weft will be in the same shed as the previous fine weft.

The front of the runner is just the opposite of the back. Treadling will bring up the bottom layer. The top layer is on shaft 1. The bottom layer is on shaft 2. (If using four shafts, the top layer will be on shafts 1 and 3. The bottom layer will be on shafts 2 and 4.)

BATHROOM RUG

Turquoise and Sand

This small rug is the perfect size for a bathroom, and in this project you'll weave enough fabric for two. I chose 6/2 unmercerized cotton for softness, but it may be hard to find. You can substitute 8/2 unmercerized cotton, although the weave will be a little looser.

MATERIALS

Finished dimensions: 20 in. x 28 in.

Warp	6/2 unmercerized cotton (WEBS): Light Aqua, Fawn, White
Weft	
fine	10/2 mercerized cotton (UKI), White
heavy	mop cotton (WEBS), White
Sett	40 epi
Reed	10 dents per inch
Sley	4 ends per dent; thread 1 end per heddle
Total ends	800
Width in reed	20 in.
Warp length	3 yd. for two rugs *(loom waste included)*
Weft sett	11 ribs (heavy only) per 2 in. (bengaline structure) 8 ribs (heavy and fine) per 2 in. (épinglé structure)
Length on loom	35.5 in. *(under tension, hems included)*
Length off loom	33 in.
Finished length	28 in. *(hemmed)*

DRESSING THE LOOM

For this project, it is preferable to dress the loom front to back—it's easier to keep track of the correct color sequence as you sley the reed. I make three color chains and sley them one at a time, carefully counting the dents and following the schematic denting draft.

Chain 1 (Light Aqua): 400 ends

Chain 2 (White): 320 ends

Chain 3 (Fawn): 80 ends

If you are weaving with two shafts, you will need 400 heddles per shaft. Remember to count your heddles before starting to dress the loom.

WARP COLOR SEQUENCE AND DENTING SCHEMATIC

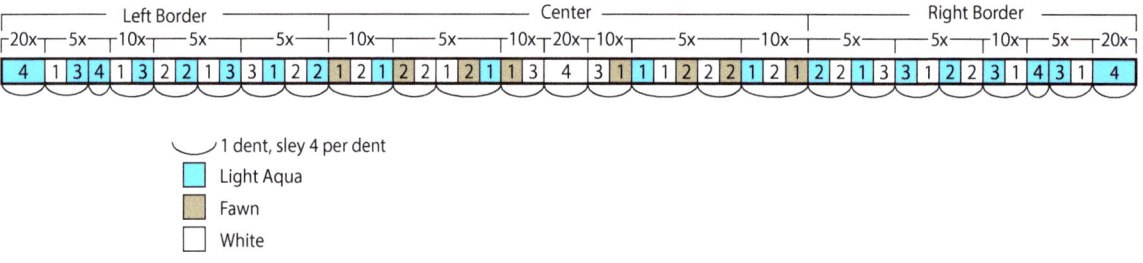

1 dent, sley 4 per dent
- Light Aqua
- Fawn
- White

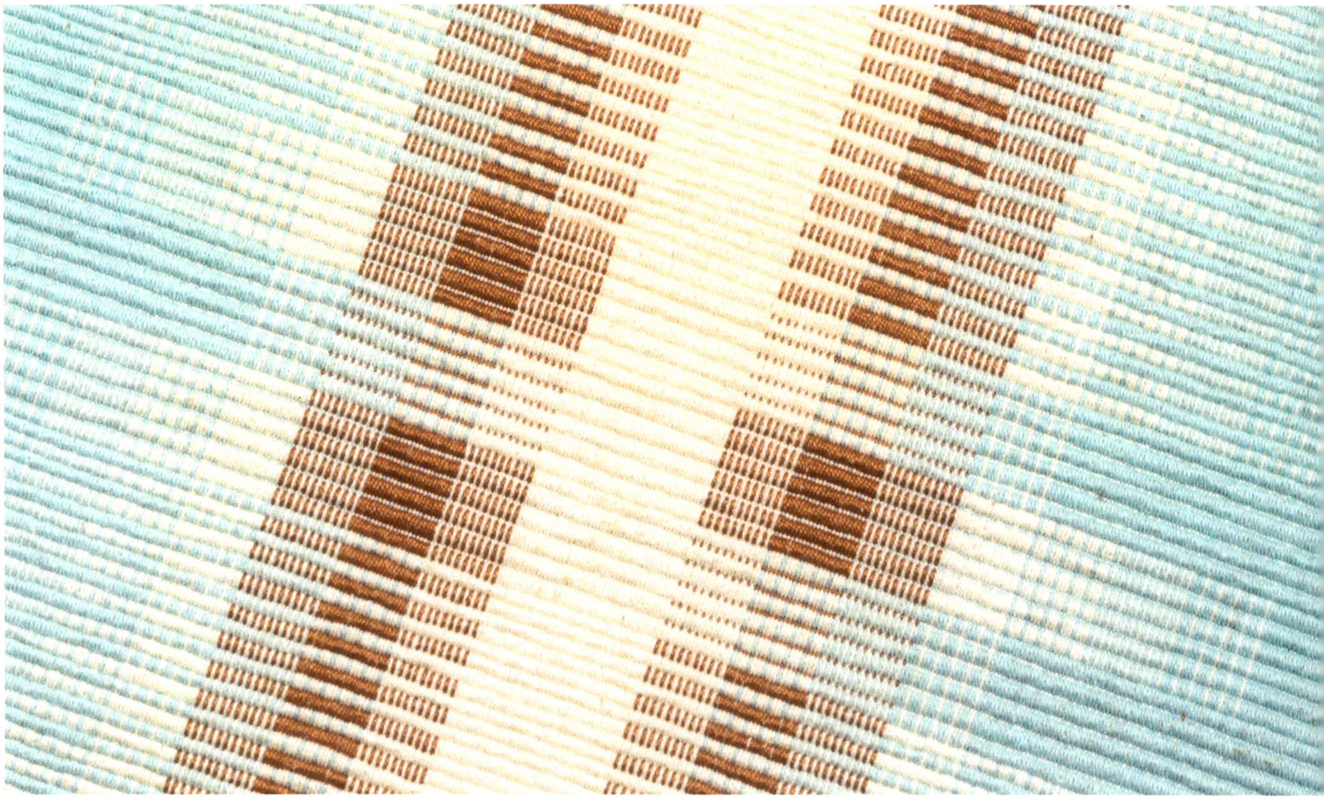

You may want to work with four shafts instead of two to make the weaving easier. Thread 1,2,3,4 instead of 1,2,1,2, as you would on two shafts. The four-shaft tie-up is 1-3, 2-4.

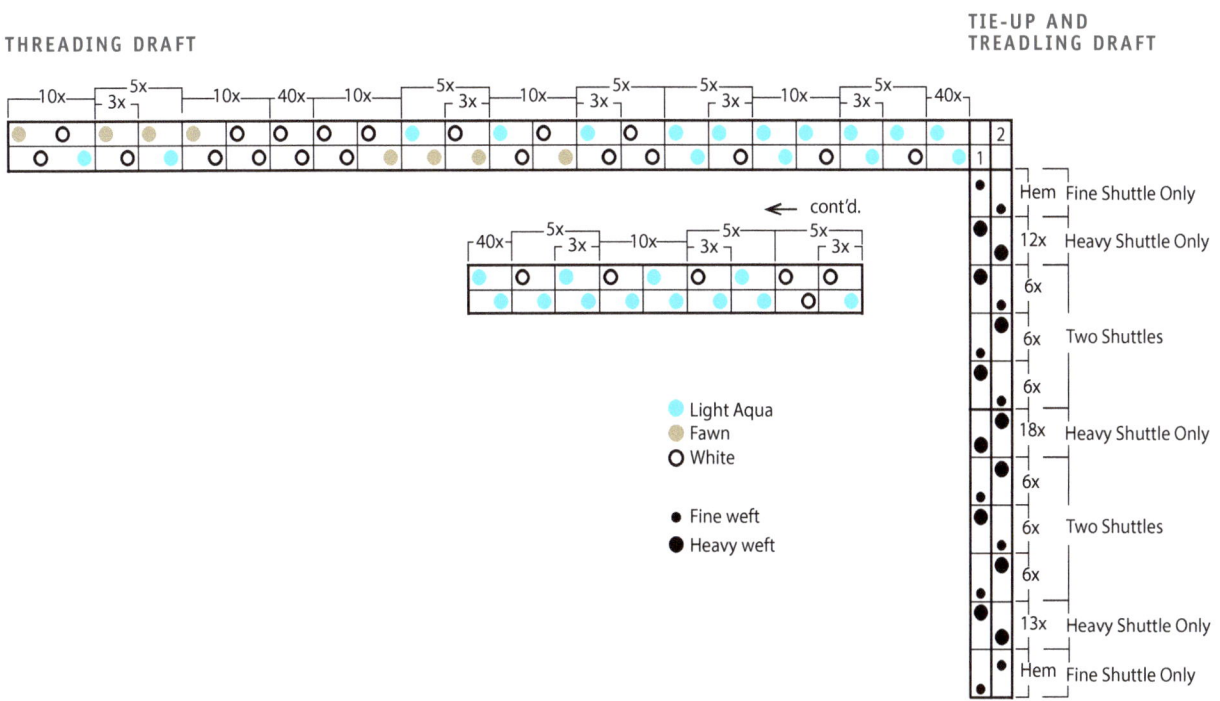

This rug combines traditional rep weave with two different weft thicknesses (a weave structure called épinglé) and a warp-faced weave with only heavy weft (a structure called bengaline).

WEAVING

Start by weaving a hem with only the fine weft for about 2 in., alternating shafts 1 and 2. Avoid arching the weft or you will get a wavy hem.

When weaving the body of the rug, follow the treadling draft, paying attention to whether you need to use one or two shuttles.

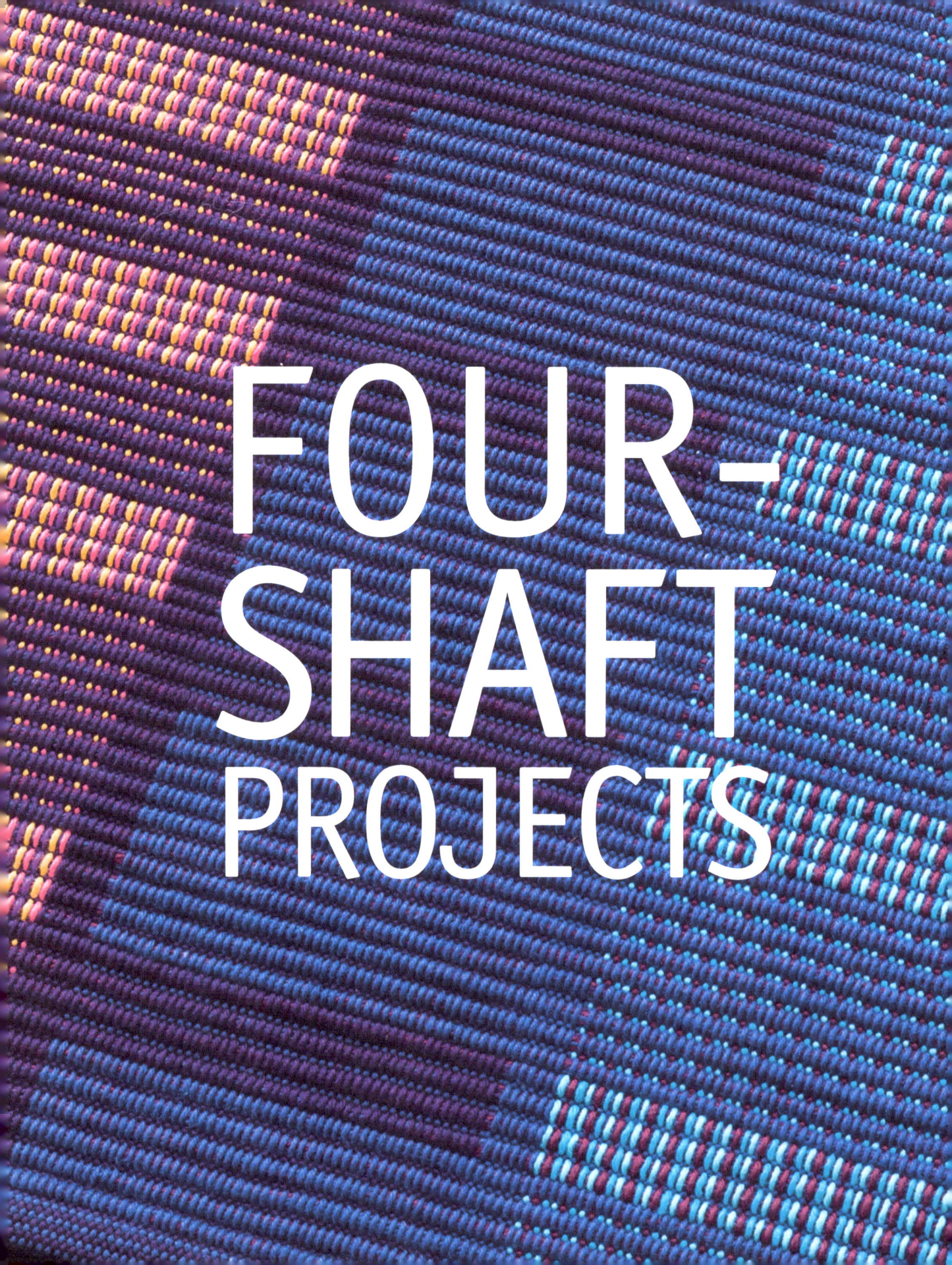

FOUR-SHAFT PROJECTS

Two-Block Patterns on Four Shafts

THE PROJECT DESIGNS in this chapter feature more two-block patterns. Because the blocks are woven on four shafts, however, they can be woven independently—which would be impossible to achieve on two shafts. With two shafts, the weaving of one block affects the other.

The "Windowpanes" placemats and runner (page 49) allow you to play with the blocks singly or in combinations. Keep in mind that there are many more variations possible than the few I show you here.

"Rail Tracks" (page 52) is a simple two-block weave pattern. It uses 8/4 carpet warp in three colors and a thicker heavy weft, made with 12 threads. To weave a firm rug, you will need to be sure that your beat is tight.

"Noël" (page 57), which introduces solid lines of color into the pattern, is a holiday runner made in shades of red and green. The "Festival of Lights" table runner (page 61) is made with the same pattern but with white and shades of blue.

The "Color Changes" placemats (page 65) are designed with different colors of weft, using a loose sett. (These placemats could also be woven on two shafts if you prefer.)

The "Dinner for Two" placemats and table runner (page 69) also have a loose sett. In this project, you'll see how you can form a big block with a regular sequence of different-colored threads. Mixing colors can be very successful, especially in contemporary-style designs.

PLACEMATS AND TABLE RUNNER

Windowpanes

This project lets you work with blocks singly or in combinations. There are many variations possible and I have presented only a few here. You can make your own design by mixing two or more treadling sequences, but keep the total number of ribs constant so your placemats will match. Sometimes the pattern will require another rib or two.

MATERIALS

Finished dimensions: placemats 12.5 in. x 16.5 in.; runner 12.5 in. x 22 in.

Warp	8/4 carpet warp (Maysville): Smokey Blue, Ivory
Weft	
fine	8/4 carpet warp (Maysville), Ivory
heavy	12 threads of 8/4 carpet warp (Maysville): 7 threads Ivory, 5 threads Smokey Blue
Sett	32 epi
Reed	8 dents per inch
Sley	4 per dent; thread 1 end per heddle
Total ends	392
Width in reed	12.5 in.
Warp length	5 yd. *(loom waste included)*
Weft sett	8 ribs (heavy and fine) per 2 in.
Length on loom	placemats 21.5 in.; runner 26.5 in. *(under tension, hems included)*
Length off loom	placemats 20.75 in; runner 25 in.
Finished length	placemats 16.5 in.; runner 22 in. *(washed, hemmed)*

PROFILE DRAFT

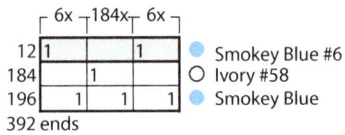

Ends per block

WARP COLOR SEQUENCE

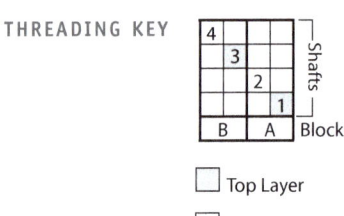

- ● Smokey Blue #6
- ○ Ivory #58
- ● Smokey Blue

392 ends

THREADING KEY

	4		
		3	
			2
				1
B	A		

Shafts / Blocks

☐ Top Layer
☐ Bottom Layer

THREADING DRAFT

● Smokey Blue
○ Ivory

∘ Fine weft
○ Heavy weft

TIE-UP AND TREADLING DRAFT

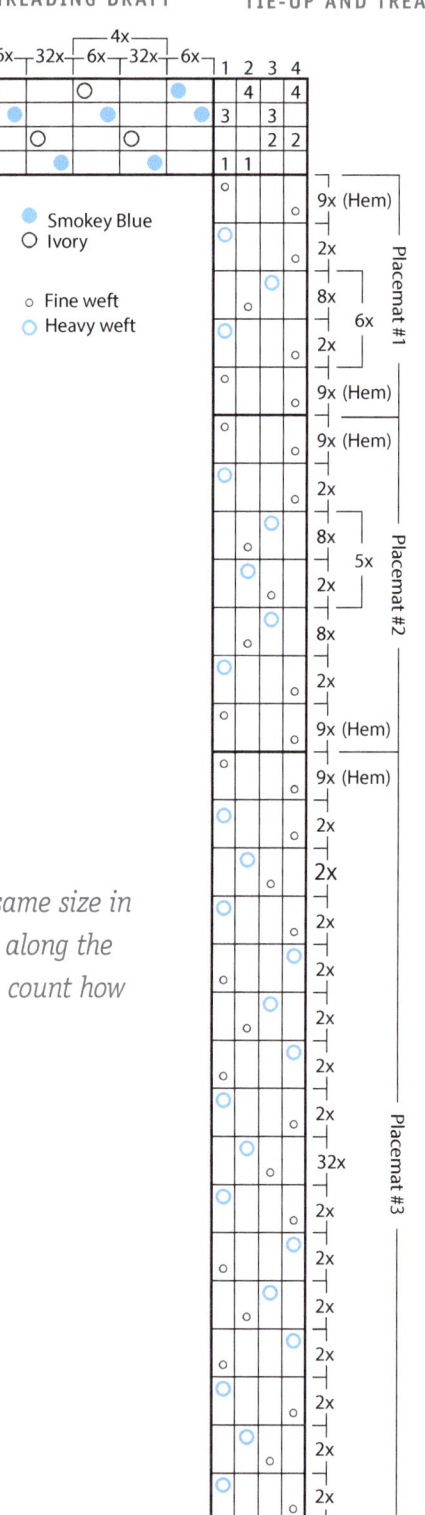

It's difficult to duplicate placemats of the same size in rep weave. I usually run a measuring tape along the side of the weaving and, at the same time, count how many ribs I have in the total length.

WEAVING

The runner and each of the placemats start with 18 shots of fine weft for the hem, using treadles 1 and 3.

Follow the treadling sequence using both wefts. Keep in mind that you may have to vary slightly the lengths (and rib count) of the finished placemats to accommodate the pattern repeat.

KITCHEN RUG

Rail Tracks

This two-block design is woven with three colors of heavyweight carpet warp. Heavy rugs like this one hold up better when finished with a hem rather than with fringe. This rug has a different threading key because the large center block is threaded on two nonadjacent shafts.

MATERIALS

Finished dimensions: 22 in. x 40 in.

Warp	8/4 carpet warp (Maysville): Velvet, Red, Tan
Weft	
fine	8/4 carpet warp (Maysville), Velvet
heavy	12 threads of 8/4 carpet warp (Maysville): 6 threads Velvet, 6 threads Red
Sett	32 epi
Reed	8 dents per inch
Sley	4 ends per dent; thread 1 end per heddle
Total ends	704
Width in reed	22 in.
Warp length	2.5 yd. *(loom waste included)*
Weft sett	7 ribs (heavy and fine) per 2 in.
Length on loom	52 in. *(under tension, with hems)*
Length off loom	47 in.
Finished length	40 in. *(hemmed)*

PROFILE DRAFT

	B	
A		A
196	312	196

Ends per block

WARP COLOR SEQUENCE

	64x	2x (3x)	2x (3x)	6x (3x)	2x	2x	156x	2x	2x	6x (3x)	2x (3x)	2x (3x)	64x	
192				1			1			1			1	Red #22
16			1			1		1			1			Tan #30
144	1	1			1				1			1	1	Velvet #84
172			1			1	1	1			1			Tan #30
16		1			1				1			1		Velvet #84
164	1			1						1			1	Red #22

704 ends

THREADING KEY

THREADING DRAFT

TIE-UP AND TREADLING DRAFT

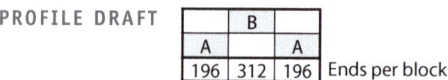

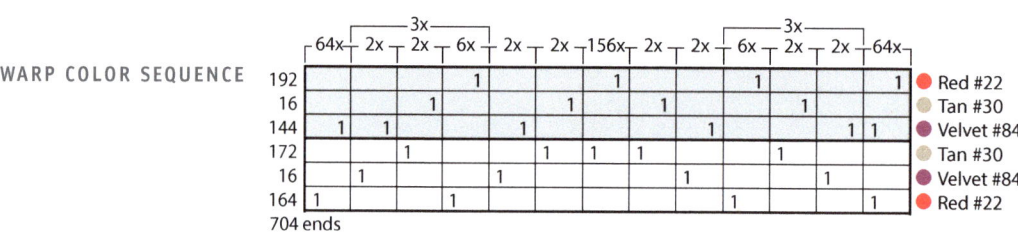

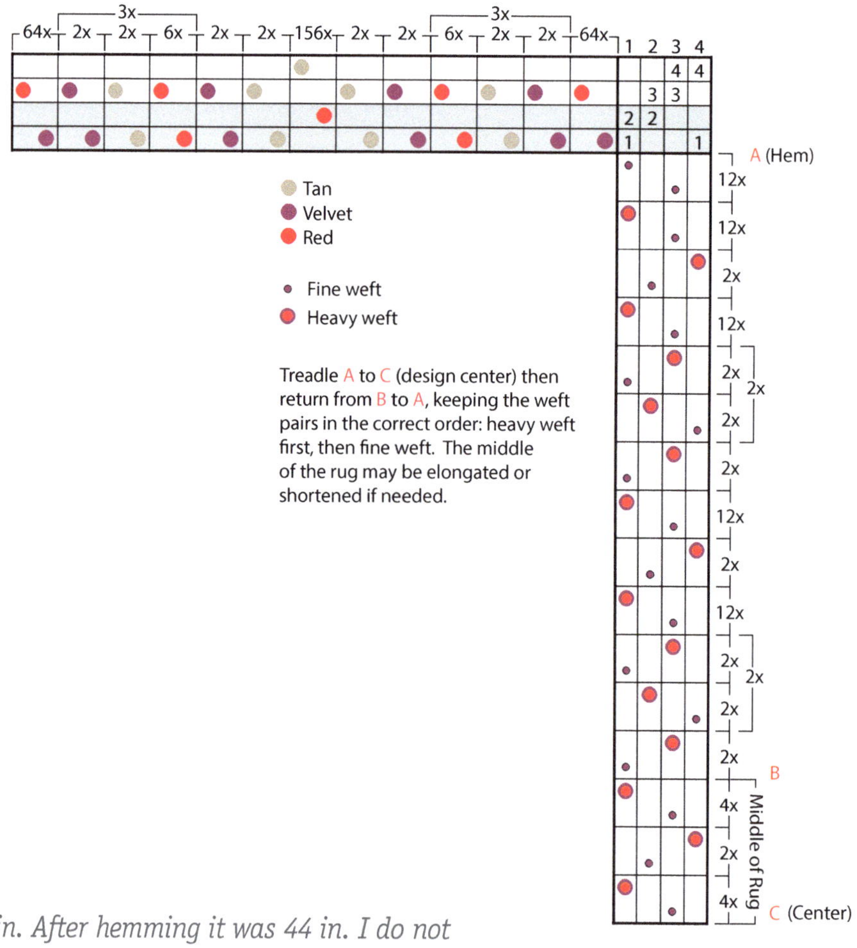

Treadle A to C (design center) then return from B to A, keeping the weft pairs in the correct order: heavy weft first, then fine weft. The middle of the rug may be elongated or shortened if needed.

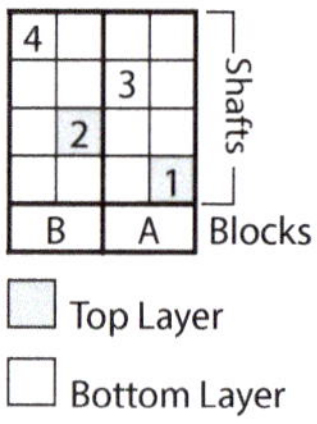

Off the loom my rug was 47 in. After hemming it was 44 in. I do not usually wash a rug after weaving, but eventually it will need to be cleaned. When I do wash it, I believe the rug will be close to the 40 in. I had originally planned.

WEAVING

Start by weaving the hem with only the fine weft for 2 in. Follow the treadling sequence with both wefts and finish with another hem.

Because of the way I weave, my rug measured 52 in. long on the loom, including hems. Keep records of your own measurements—your beat and the tension of the warp are important factors in determining the finished length. Keep in mind that off the loom the rug may relax and reduce up to 17 percent in length.

As you can see in the threading key, Block A is not threaded on adjacent shafts. This threading makes it easier to weave large blocks with a large number of threads, like the one at the center of this design (Block B).

TABLE RUNNER

Noël

This holiday table runner introduces solid lines of color at the borders of the block design. The solid lines are made with light-orange cotton warp threads but you could substitute a strong metallic thread instead.

MATERIALS

Finished dimensions: 13.5 in. x 38 in.

Warp	5/2 pearl cotton (UKI): Forest, Mountain, Wine, Red, Light Orange
Weft	
fine	5/2 pearl cotton or 10/2 mercerized cotton (UKI), Red
heavy	12 threads of 5/2 pearl cotton (UKI): 6 threads Wine, 6 threads Red
Sett	40 epi
Reed	10 dents per inch
Sley	4 ends per dent, thread 1 end per heddle
Total ends	544
Width in reed	13.6 in.
Warp length	2.5 yd.
Weft sett	8 ribs (heavy and fine) per 2 in.
Length on loom	45 in. *(under tension, hems included)*
Length off loom	43 in.
Finished length	39 in. *(washed, hemmed)*

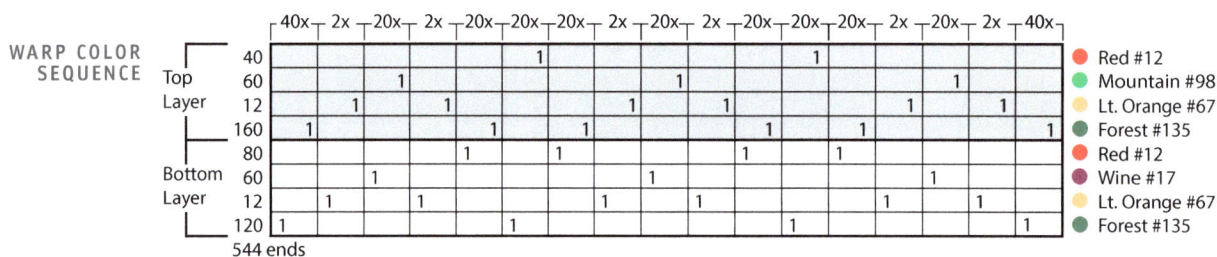

The warp threads that make up the solid lines in the design are threaded on the same pair of shafts as the adjacent block.

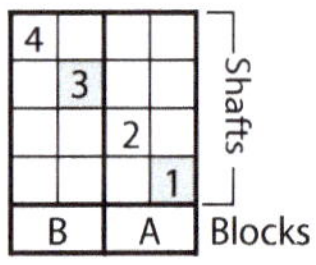

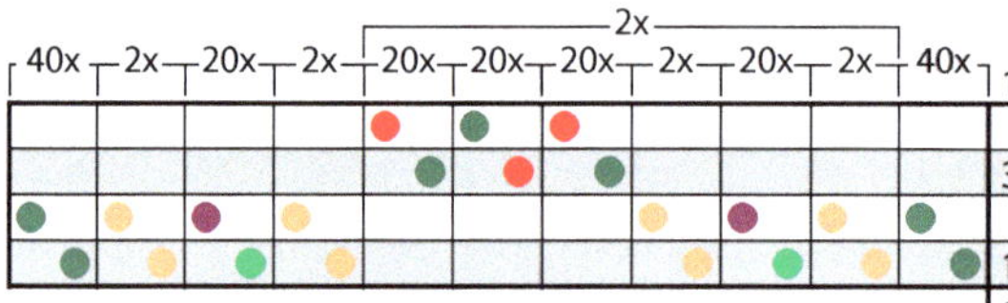

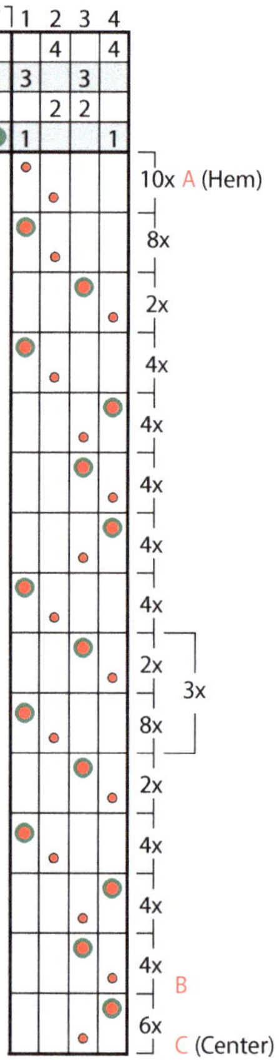

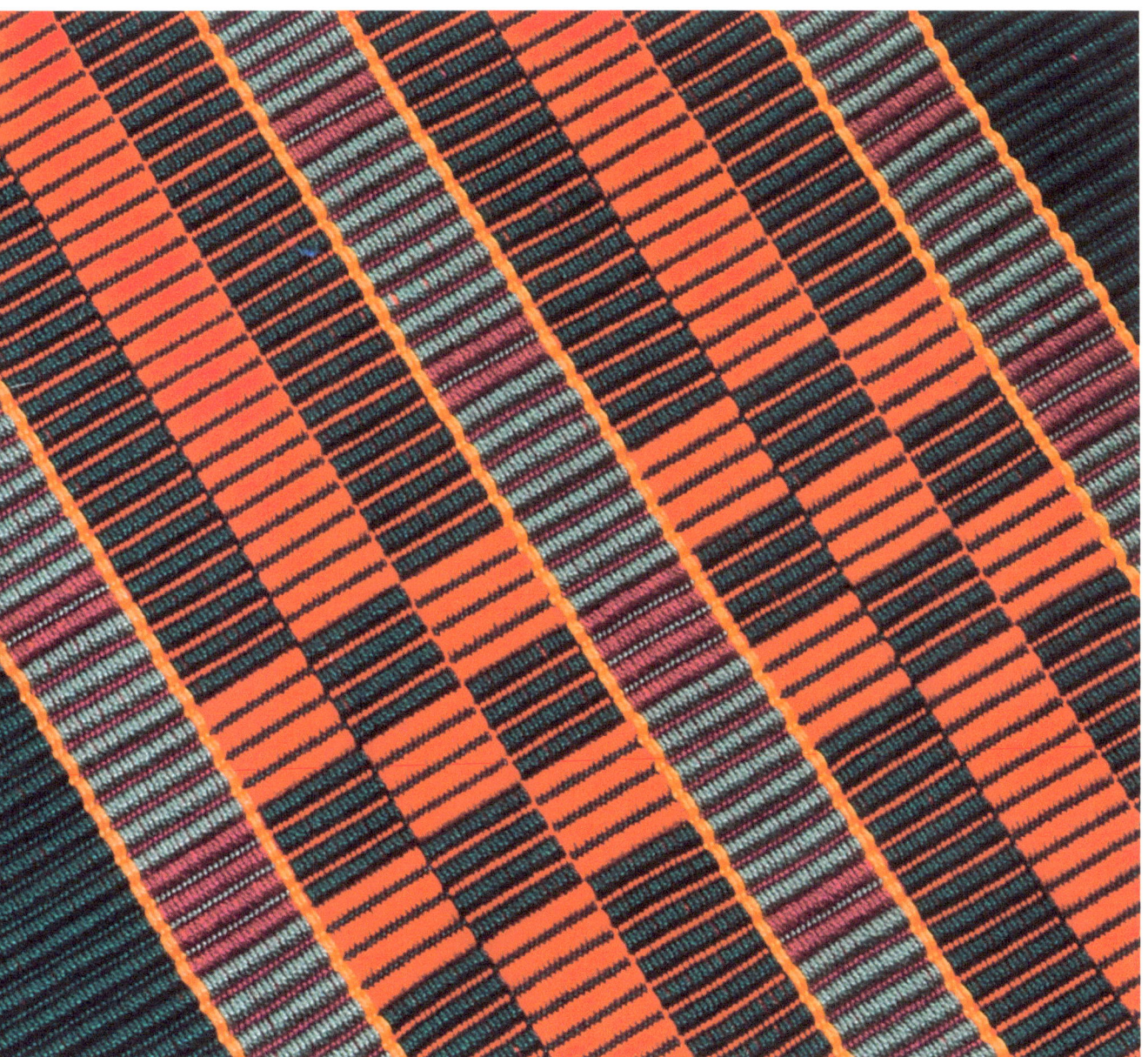

WEAVING

Start by weaving a hem with the fine weft, using treadles 1 and 2. Follow the treadling sequence, working with both shuttles. Keep in mind that when you switch to another treadling block, the heavy weft shot may be in the same shed as the previous fine shot—which will not affect the weaving and will help you keep the shuttles rotating in the correct sequence.

You can make many variations of this runner by changing the proportions. Although I usually try to match the color of the weft to the color of the edge block, for this design I used a heavy weft made of red ends of varying shades to create a decorative effect at the selvedge ends.

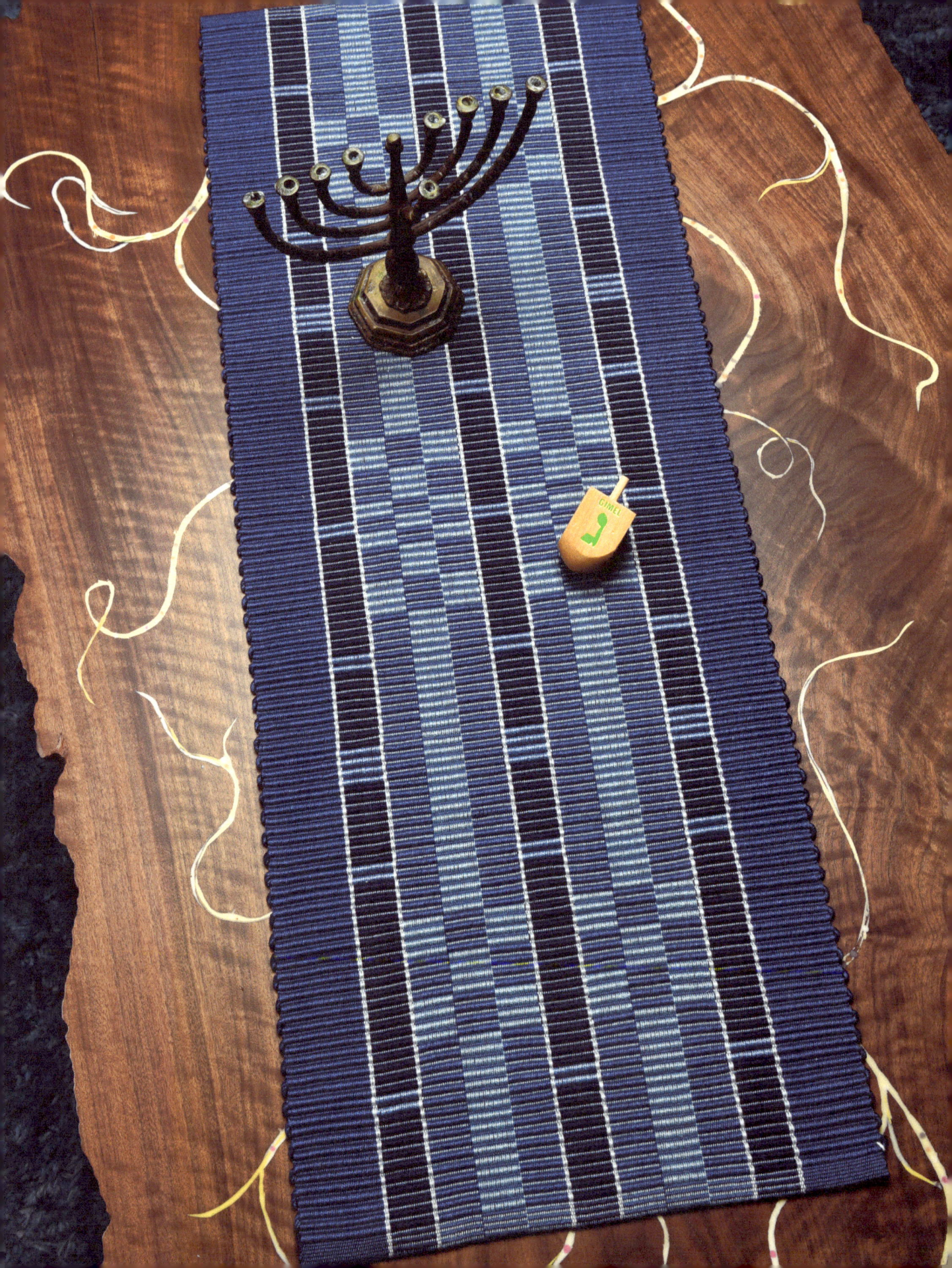

TABLE RUNNER

Festival of Lights

This table runner, designed for Hanukkah celebrations, is a variation on the Noël table runner (page 57). You could make the solid lines of color that border the blocks (shown here in the UKI color Stone) with a silver metallic thread instead.

MATERIALS

Finished dimensions: 13.5 in. x 36 in.

Warp	5/2 pearl cotton (UKI): Soldier Blue, Deep Purple, Mineral, Copen, Stone
Weft	
fine	10/2 mercerized cotton (UKI), Black
heavy	12 threads of 5/2 pearl cotton (UKI): mix of Soldier Blue and Deep Purple
Sett	40 epi
Reed	10 dents per inch
Sley	4 ends per dent; thread 1 end per heddle
Total ends	544
Width in reed	13.6 in.
Warp length	2.5 yd. *(loom waste included)*
Weft sett	8 ribs (heavy and fine) per 2 in.
Length on loom	41 in. *(under tension, hems included)*
Length off loom	39 in.
Finished length	36 in. *(washed, hemmed)*

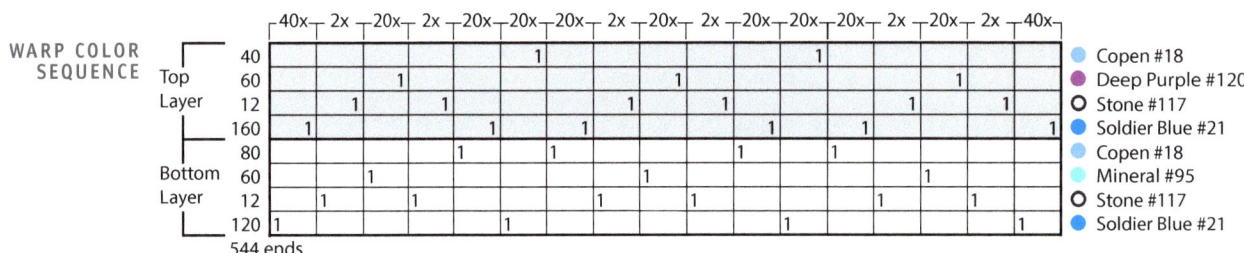

PROFILE DRAFT

A	B	A	B	A
128	120	48	120	128

Ends per block

WARP COLOR SEQUENCE

544 ends

- Copen #18
- Deep Purple #120
- Stone #117
- Soldier Blue #21
- Copen #18
- Mineral #95
- Stone #117
- Soldier Blue #21

THREADING KEY

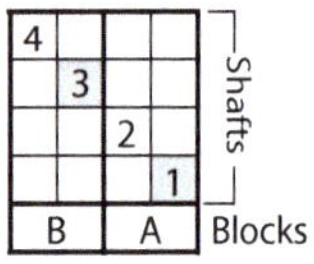

Top Layer
Bottom Layer

THREADING DRAFT

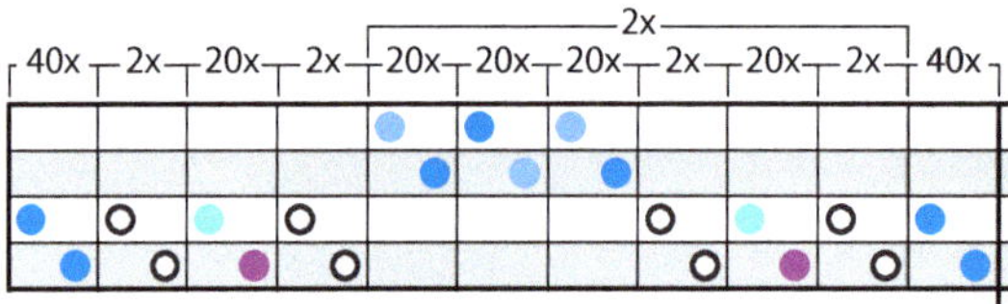

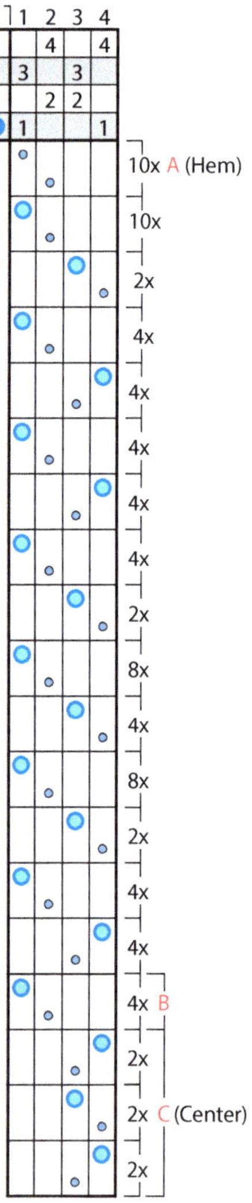

- Deep Purple
- Copen
- Mineral
- Stone
- Soldier Blue

- Fine weft
- Heavy weft

Treadle A to C (design center) then from B to A, keeping the weft pairs in the correct order: heavy weft first, then fine weft.

TIE-UP AND TREADLING DRAFT

10x A (Hem)
10x
2x
4x
4x
4x
4x
4x
2x
8x
4x
8x
2x
4x
4x
4x B
2x
2x C (Center)
2x

Be sure to sample the heavy weft blocks so you will have perfectly balanced squares.

WEAVING

Start by weaving a hem with the fine weft. Follow the treadling sequence, working with both shuttles. Keep in mind that when you switch to another treadling block, the heavy weft shot may be in the same shed as the previous fine shot—which will not affect the weaving and will help you keep the shuttles rotating in the correct sequence.

As with the "Noël" runner, you can make many variations of this runner by changing the proportions. I used dark blue and purple for the heavy weft and light blue for the solid lines bordering the blocks on each side of the piece.

PLACEMATS

Color Changes

This project is woven with different colors of weft and a loose sett. The variations in the weft colors changes the entire look of the four individual placemats. (You could also weave these placemats on two shafts.)

MATERIALS

Finished dimensions: 12 in. x 18 in.

Warp	8/4 carpet warp (Maysville): Eggplant, Purple, Lavender, Pale Blue
Weft	
fine	10/2 mercerized cotton (UKI), Black
heavy	10 strands of 8/4 carpet warp (Maysville): different color combinations
Sett	20 epi
Reed	10 dents per inch
Sley	2 ends per dent; thread 1 end per heddle
Total ends	248
Width in reed	12.4 in.
Warp length	3.5 yd. for four placemats *(loom waste included)*
Weft sett	8 ribs (heavy and fine) per 2 in.
Length on loom	22 in. *(under tension, hems included)*
Length off loom	20 in.
Finished length	18 in. *(washed, hemmed)*

In projects like this one, color is important. Try making your weft with your warp colors—or with only dark colors or light ones. Don't be afraid to experiment. Be bold!

WARP COLOR SEQUENCE

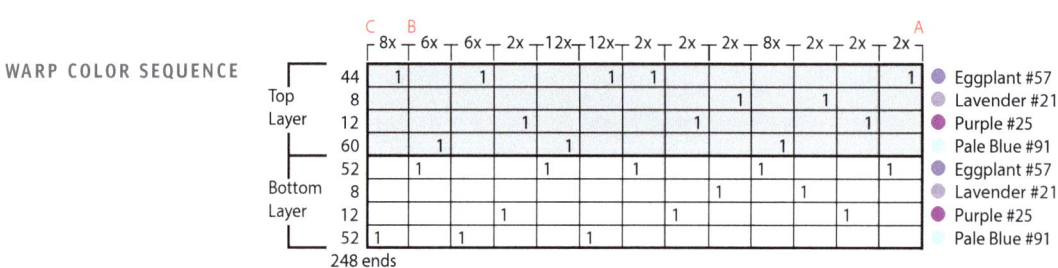

Wind warp holding one thread from the bottom layer and one from the top layer keeping the threads separate with your fingers. Warp A to C and return B to A.

DENTING SCHEMATIC

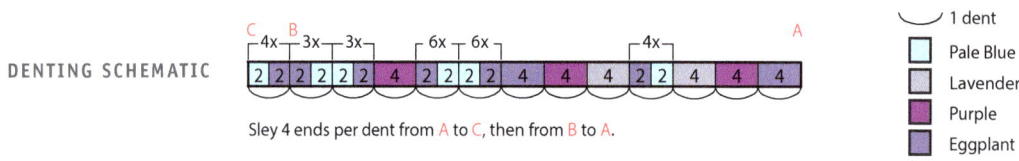

Sley 4 ends per dent from A to C, then from B to A.

THREADING DRAFT

TIE-UP AND TREADLING DRAFT

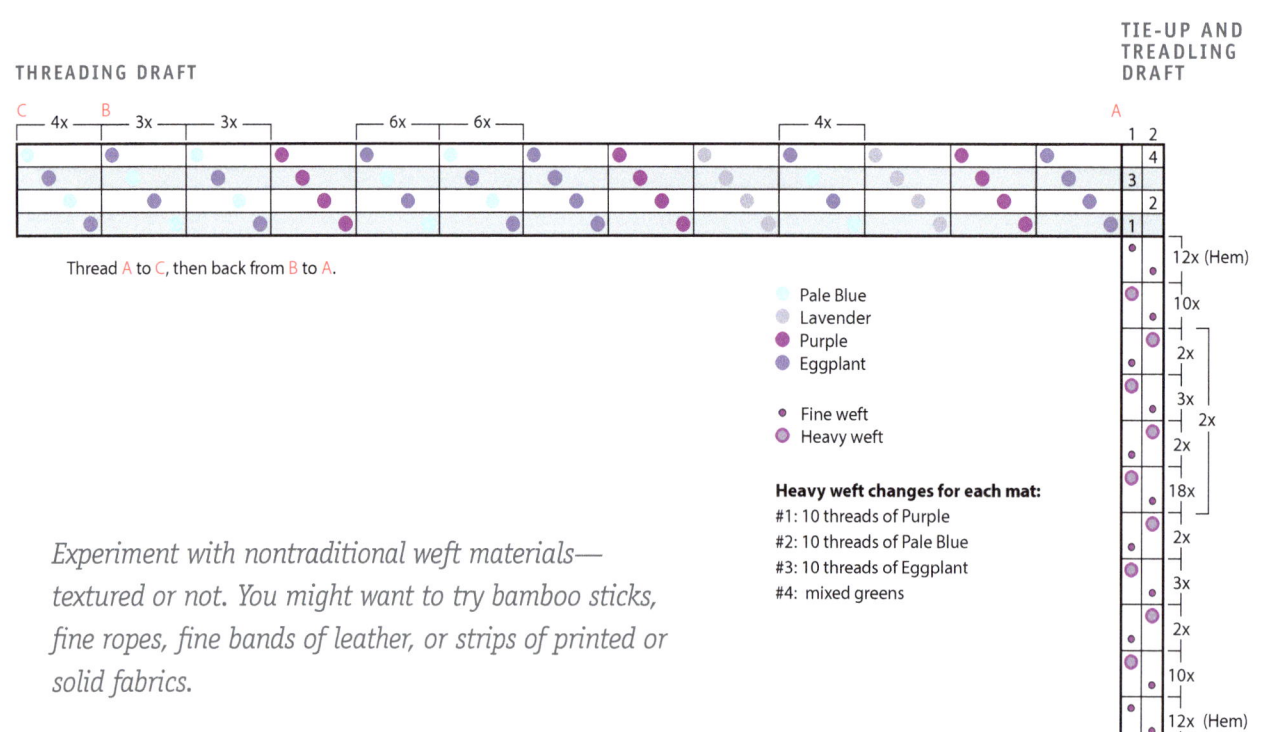

Thread A to C, then back from B to A.

- Pale Blue
- Lavender
- Purple
- Eggplant

• Fine weft
○ Heavy weft

Heavy weft changes for each mat:
#1: 10 threads of Purple
#2: 10 threads of Pale Blue
#3: 10 threads of Eggplant
#4: mixed greens

Experiment with nontraditional weft materials— textured or not. You might want to try bamboo sticks, fine ropes, fine bands of leather, or strips of printed or solid fabrics.

WEAVING

Start by weaving a hem with the fine weft, using treadles 1 and 2. Follow the treadling sequence, working with both shuttles.

All the placemats follow the same treadling sequence. I restricted myself to just changing color in the heavy wefts. I mostly used the warp colors but I also brought in a completely different color—green.

The change in weft color created a subtle variation in the finished piece but it also affected the lengths of the mats, even though they were all woven and finished the same way. The shrinkage in these placemats was much greater than usual, both because of the loose sett and the heavy carpet warp thread.

PLACEMATS AND TABLE RUNNER

Dinner for Two

These colorful placemats feature two very large blocks at each long edge of the fabric. Instead of using a single color for the pattern layer, the large blocks are made with three different-colored warp threads in a repeated sequence. This project includes two placemats and a table runner.

MATERIALS

Finished dimensions: placemats 12.5 in. x 18 in.; runner 12.5 in. x 31 in.

Warp	8/4 carpet warp (Maysville): Navy Blue, Eggplant, Purple, Gold, Tulip, Light Jade, Velvet, Parakeet
Weft	
fine	8/4 carpet warp (Maysville), Navy Blue
heavy	10 strands of 8/4 carpet warp (Maysville): mix of Navy Blue and Eggplant
Sett	24 epi
Reed	12 dents per inch
Sley	2 ends per dent; thread 1 end per heddle
Total ends	312
Width in reed	13 in.
Warp length	4 yd. for two placemats and a table runner *(loom waste included)*
Weft sett	10 ribs (heavy and fine) per 2 in.
Length on loom	placemats 22 in.; runner 37 in. *(under tension, hems included)*
Length off loom	placemats 20 in.; runner 34 in.
Finished length	placemats 18 in.; runner 31 in. *(washed, hemmed)*

PROFILE DRAFT

B		B		
	A		A	
108	96	12	96	Ends per block

WARP COLOR SEQUENCE

		16x			6x	48x	6x	16x			
Top Layer	54	1	1	1	1						Eggplant #57
	102					1	1	1	1	1	Navy Blue #5
Bottom Layer	16	1									Purple #25
	16		1								Gold #10
	16			1							Tulip #51
	54				1	1					Eggplant #57
	6						1				Navy Blue #5
	16							1			Light Jade #37
	16								1		Velvet #84
	16									1	Parakeet #48
	312 ends										

THREADING DRAFT

TIE-UP AND TREADLING DRAFT

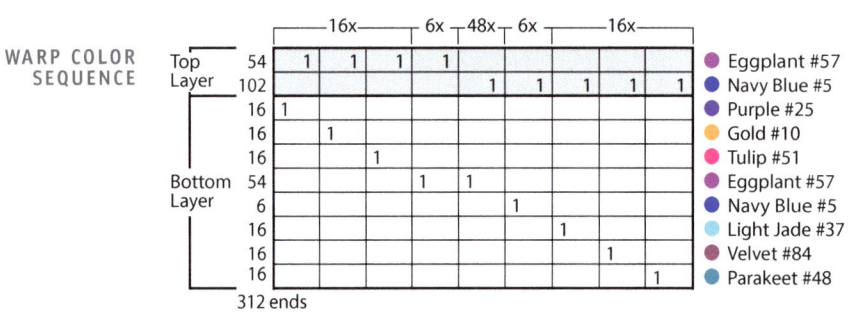

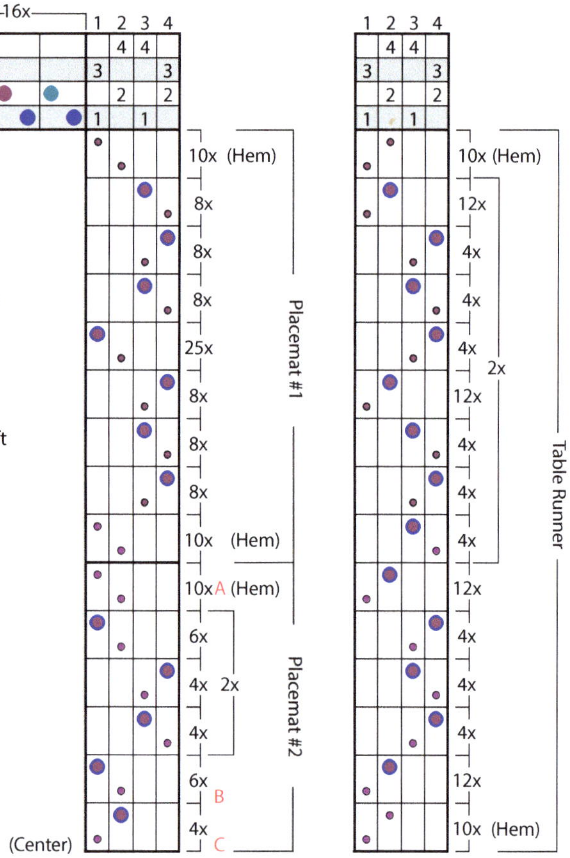

Placemat #2:
Treadle A to C (design center) then from B to A, keeping the weft pairs in the correct order: heavy weft first, then fine weft.

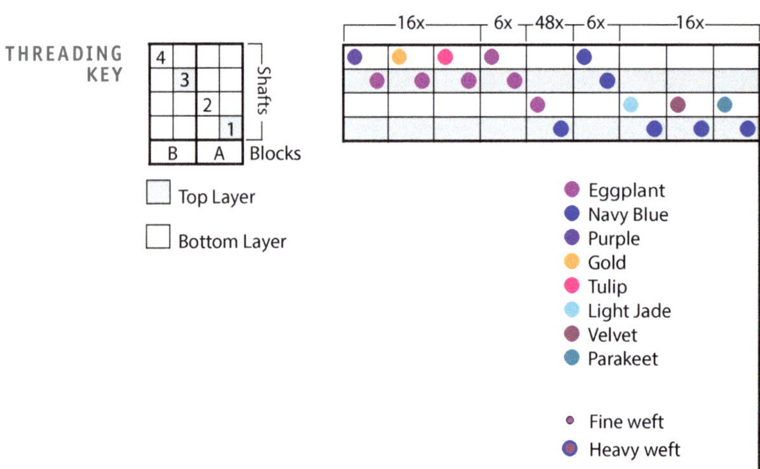

If you want to add two more placemats, increase the warp length to 5½ yd.

WEAVING

Start by weaving the hem. Then follow the treadling sequence. I am presenting two different treadling sequences for the placemats and one for the runner.

The warp for this project has a loose sett, which means the weft will be visible in the finished fabric. The loose sett also explains the high rate of length shrinkage.

Four-Block Patterns on Four Shafts

FOR THE PROJECTS in this section, you'll work with four shafts to create four-block patterns. The two sets of blocks (A, B and C, D) share the same shaft pairs but in reverse order—for example:

Block A: Shaft 1 for background, Shaft 2 for pattern
Block B: Shaft 3 for background, Shaft 4 for pattern

Block C: Shaft 2 for background, Shaft 1 for pattern
Block D: Shaft 4 background, Shaft 3 for pattern

Be careful of the transition between blocks—especially between blocks that use the same pair of shafts (Blocks A and C; Blocks B and D). When adjacent threads rise together, a line forms on the top surface of the weaving, leaving a space underneath. This line is unavoidable and is a characteristic of rep weave.

The first project ("Navajo Traditions," page 75) is a sampler that will help you understand how the blocks are woven together.

"Theme Variations" (page 79) introduces blocks of different widths arranged in sequence. This project also introduces a new style of threading key and another drafting method. The "Adding Colors" table runner and placemats (page 83) have the same drafts as "Theme Variations," but there are more colors, which creates a very different appearance.

"Five Shades of Gray" (page 87) features a new way of making the warp. Using two ends of fine warp thread, you'll make one "working end." The working end passes through one dent and one heddle as if a single thread. The warps for many Swedish designs are prepared this way because the double thread provides better weft coverage.

SAMPLER

Navajo Traditions

This long sampler will help you understand how four patterned blocks weave together on four shafts. You can enlarge the drafts for any one of the four block patterns to make placemats, a table runner, a rug, or a wall hanging. I used a black background to create strong contrast.

MATERIALS

Finished dimensions: 8 in. x 48 in. (excluding fringe)

Warp	3/2 mercerized cotton (WEBS): Black, Alabaster, Amber Gold, Golden Ochre, Madder Brown
Weft	
fine	10/2 mercerized cotton (WEBS), Black
heavy	8 threads of 3/2 cotton (WEBS), Black
Sett	32 epi
Reed	8 dents per inch
Sley	four ends per dent; thread 1 end per heddle
Total ends	256
Width in reed	8 in.
Warp length	3 yd. *(loom waste included)*
Weft sett	7 ribs (heavy and fine) per 2 in.
Length on loom	52 in., depending on block hem lengths *(under tension, sample hems and fringe included)*
Length off loom	48 in.
Finished length	48 in. *(unwashed, fringe excluded)*

PROFILE DRAFT

				D			D							
		C			C	C			C			C		
	B		B					B		B			B	
A					A						A			A
24	16	16	16	16	16	16	16	16	16	16	16	16	16	24	Ends per block

WARP COLOR SEQUENCE

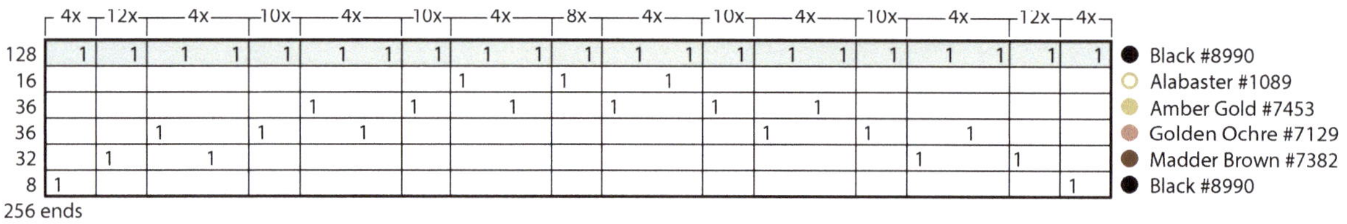

	4x	12x	4x	10x	4x	10x	4x	8x	4x	10x	4x	10x	4x	12x	4x	
128	1	1	1	1	1	1	1	1	1	1	1	1	1	1	1	● Black #8990
16						1		1		1						○ Alabaster #1089
36				1		1		1		1		1				● Amber Gold #7453
36		1		1								1		1		● Golden Ochre #7129
32	1		1										1		1	● Madder Brown #7382
8	1														1	● Black #8990

256 ends

THREADING KEY

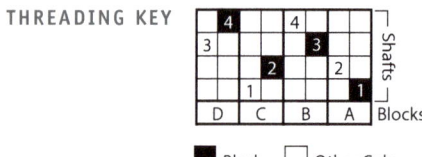

Black   ☐ Other Colors

THREADING DRAFT

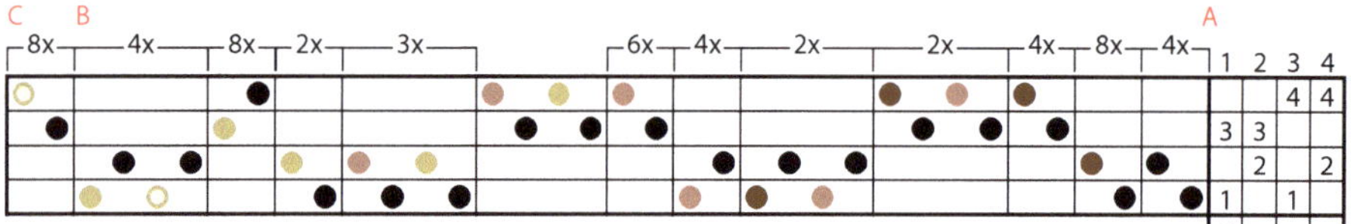

Thread A to C (design center) then return from B to A.

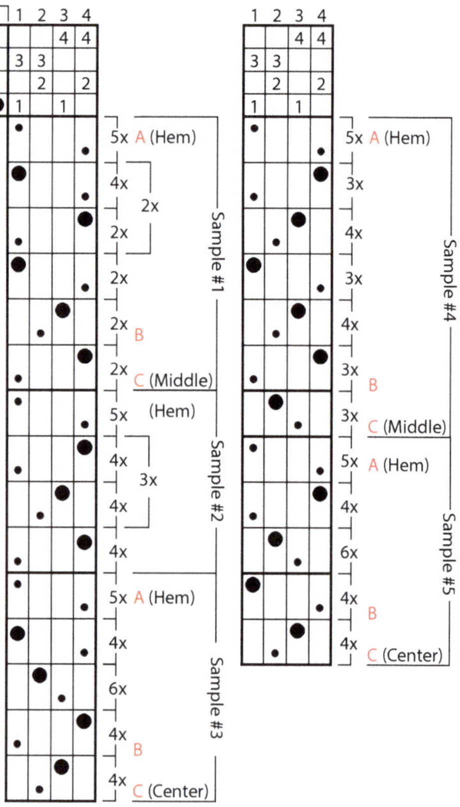

- ● Black
- ○ Alabaster
- ● Amber Gold
- ● Golden Ochre
- ● Madder Brown

- · Fine weft
- ● Heavy weft

For Samples, 1, 3, 4 and 5, treadle A to C (design center) then from B to A, keeping the weft pairs in the correct order: heavy weft first, then fine weft.

The hem areas are the separations between samples.

TIE-UP AND TREADLING DRAFT

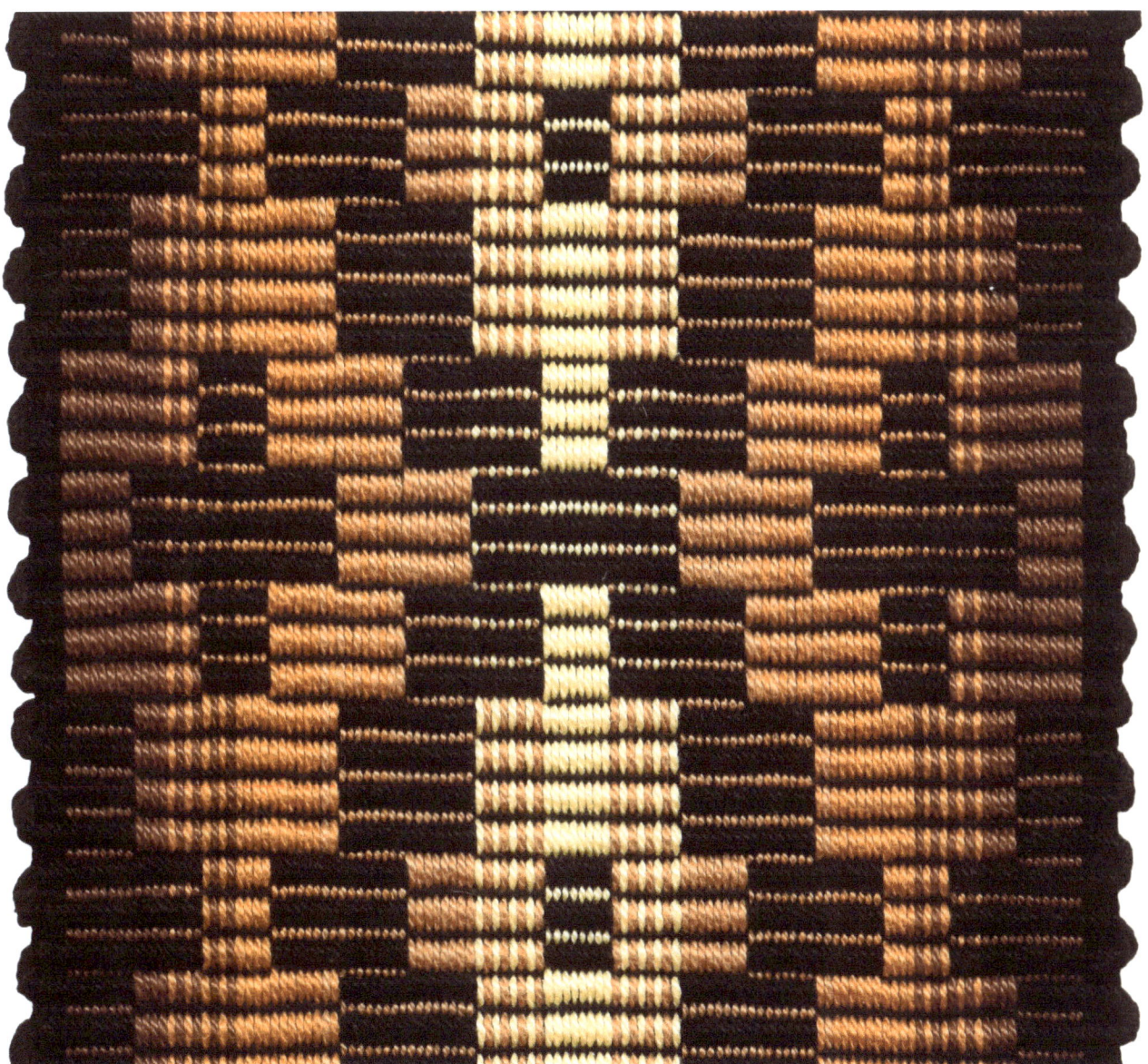

WEAVING

For this sampler, there are five different treadling sequences, corresponding to the individual samples, reading the photo on page 74 from top to bottom. When beginning each new treadling sequence, always start with a small hem area (about 10 shots of fine weft) to separate the individual sample blocks from each other.

You will notice quite often that the last fine-weft shot will lie in the same shed as the next shot of heavy weft. Don't worry. Having two shots in the same shed will not alter the blocks—in fact they are important in helping you keep the shuttles rotating in the correct sequence.

I finished this sampler with twisted fringes and hung it in my classroom. The fringe adds weight and decorative detail.

PLACEMATS AND TABLE RUNNER

Theme Variations

Each of the pieces in this project features a different design made with the same three warp colors. The unique effects resulted from varying the widths of the blocks and the sequence in which they are arranged. Choose the treadling you prefer.

MATERIALS

Finished dimensions: placemats 11.5 in. x 18.5 in.; table runner 11.5 in. x 22 in.

Warp	5/2 mercerized cotton (UKI): Dark Sierra, Paradise, Phosphate
Weft	
fine	10/2 mercerized cotton (UKI), Black
heavy	12 strands of 5/2 mercerized cotton (UKI), Dark Sierra
Sett	40 epi
Reed	10 dents per inch
Sley	4 ends per dent; thread 1 end per heddle
Total ends	476
Width in reed	11.9 in.
Warp length	5 yd. for four placemats and a table runner *(loom waste included)*
Weft sett	7 ribs (heavy and fine) per 2 in.
Length on loom	placemats 22 in.; runner 26 in. *(under tension, hems included)*
Length off loom	placemats 20 in.; runner 25.5 in.
Finished length	placemats 18.5 in.; runner 22 in. *(washed, hemmed)*

PROFILE DRAFT

	Border						Center					Border						
D		D		D		D						D		D		D		D
	C		C		C								C		C		C	
							B			B								
						A		A			A							
52	24	12	12	12	24	32	40	24	12	24	40	32	24	12	12	12	24	52	Ends per block

WARP COLOR SEQUENCE

Border — Center — Border

16x, 4x, 16x, 12x, 6x, 6x, 6x, 12x, 16x, 20x, 12x, 6x, 12x, 20x, 16x, 12x, 6x, 6x, 6x, 12x, 16x, 4x, 16x

- 112 Paradise #105
- 114 Phosphate #123
- 250 Dark Sierra #25

476 ends

WEAVING

There are three different treadling sequences for the placemats and one for the table runner. Start each placemat and the runner with a hem made with the fine weft only.

Keep track of the number of ribs per placemat and use a measuring tape to check length, too. Note that Placemat #1 has two extra ribs to accommodate the design, which makes it ¼ in. longer than the other.

THREADING KEY

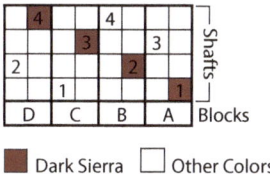

4
4
3
3
2
2
1
1
D C B A
Shafts
Blocks
Dark Sierra
Other Colors

This project has a different threading key than is usual for four blocks on four shafts. Each block is threaded on two shafts that are not adjacent. Compare it to the key in "Navajo Traditions," page 76, for example.

THREADING DRAFT

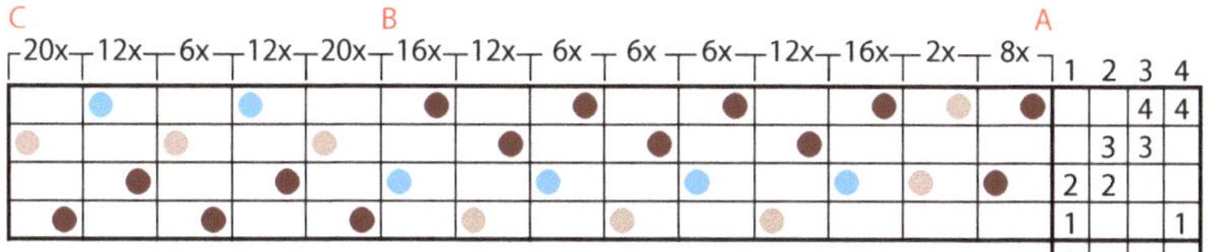

C
B
A
20x 12x 6x 12x 20x 16x 12x 6x 6x 6x 12x 16x 2x 8x

Thread A to B (border) to C (design center), then from B to A.

- Paradise
- Phosphate
- Dark Sierra

- Fine weft
- Heavy weft

Treadle A to C (design center) then from B to A, keeping the weft pairs in the correct order: heavy weft first, then fine weft.

TIE-UP AND TREADLING DRAFT

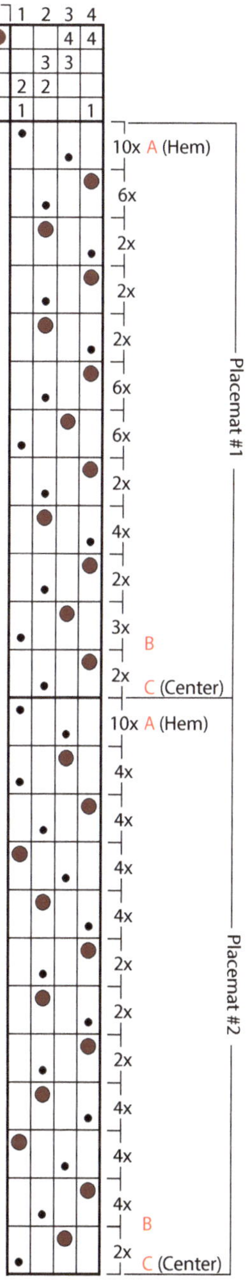

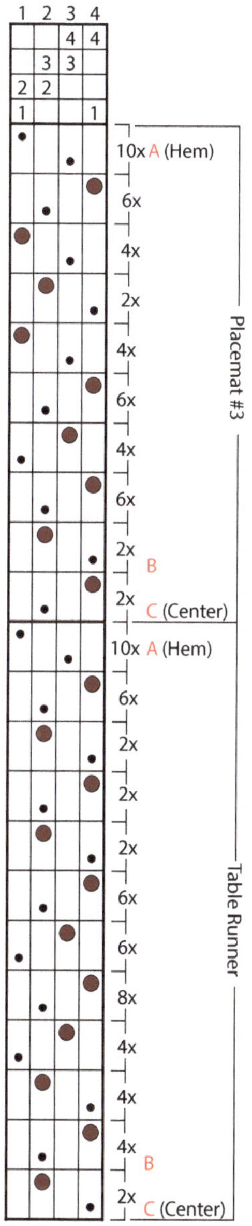

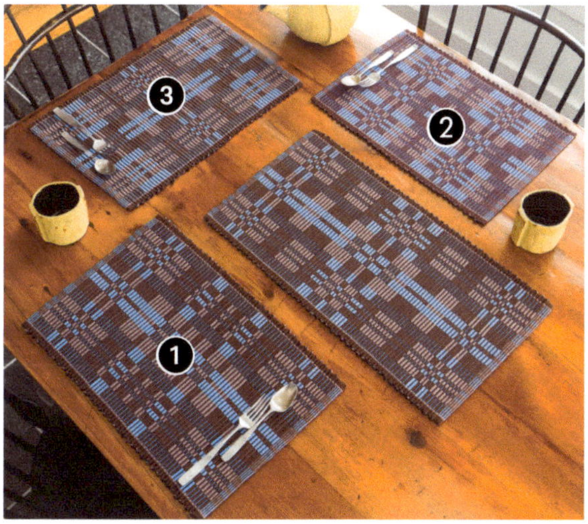

1 2 3 4
10x A (Hem)
6x
2x
2x
2x
6x
6x
2x
4x
2x
3x
B
2x
C (Center)
Placemat #1
10x A (Hem)
4x
4x
4x
4x
2x
2x
2x
4x
4x
4x
B
2x
C (Center)
Placemat #2

1 2 3 4
10x A (Hem)
6x
4x
2x
4x
6x
4x
6x
2x
B
2x
C (Center)
Placemat #3
10x A (Hem)
6x
2x
2x
2x
6x
6x
8x
4x
4x
4x
B
2x
C (Center)
Table Runner

3
2
1

TABLE RUNNER AND PLACEMATS

Adding Colors

This project is woven with the same threading as "Theme Variations" (page 79) but it has more color (therefore a different warp color sequence) and a very different finished look. This project includes the table runner shown on the facing page and four matching placemats.

MATERIALS

Finished dimensions: 12 in. x 22 in.

Warp	5/2 mercerized cotton (UKI): Sequoia, Peacock, Dark Sierra, Dusty Coral, Mineral
Weft	
fine	10/2 mercerized cotton (UKI), Black
heavy	12 threads of 5/2 mercerized cotton (UKI): 6 threads Sequoia, 6 threads Dark Sierra
Sett	40 epi
Reed	10 dents per inch
Sley	4 ends per dent; thread 1 end per heddle
Total ends	476
Width in reed	11.9 in.
Warp length	5 yd. for four placemats and a runner *(loom waste included)*
Weft sett	7 ribs (heavy and fine) per 2 in.
Length on loom	25 in. *(under tension, hems included)*
Length off loom	23 in.
Finished length	22 in. *(washed, hemmed)*

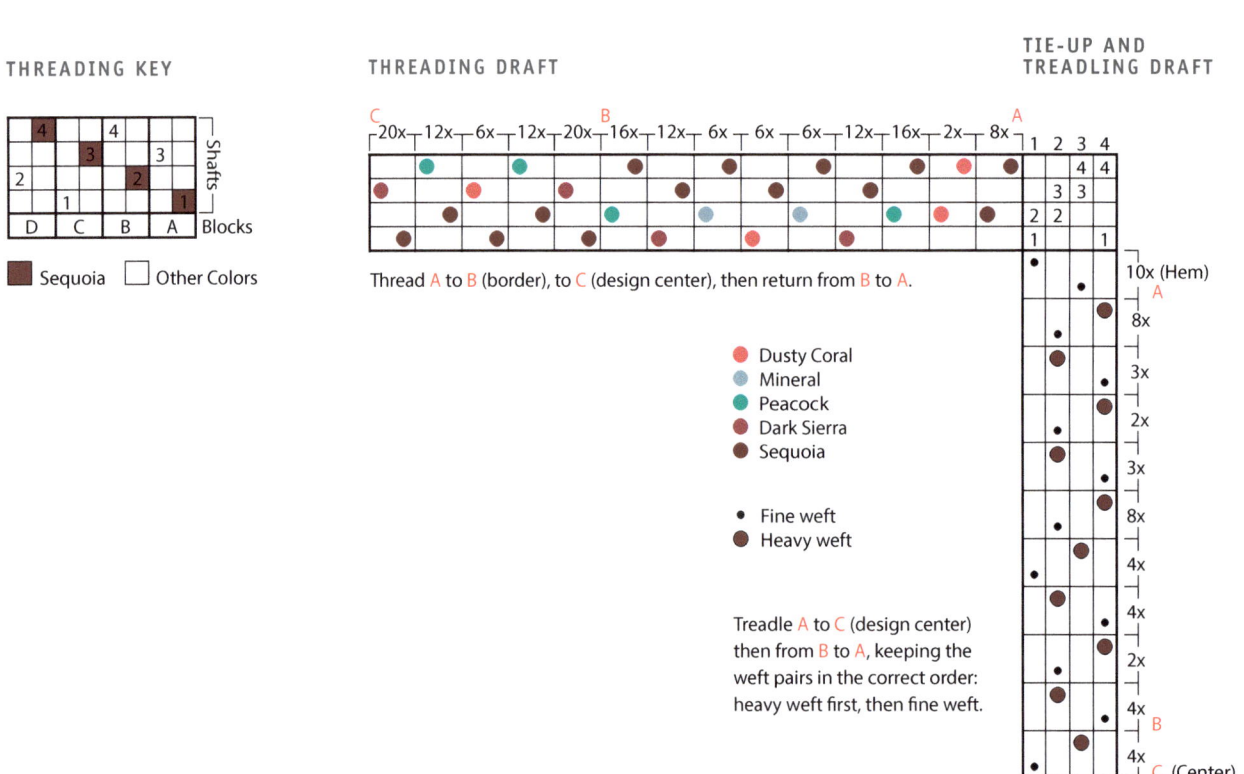

This project, like "Theme Variations," has a different threading key than is usually used for four blocks on four shafts. Each block is threaded on two nonadjacent shafts.

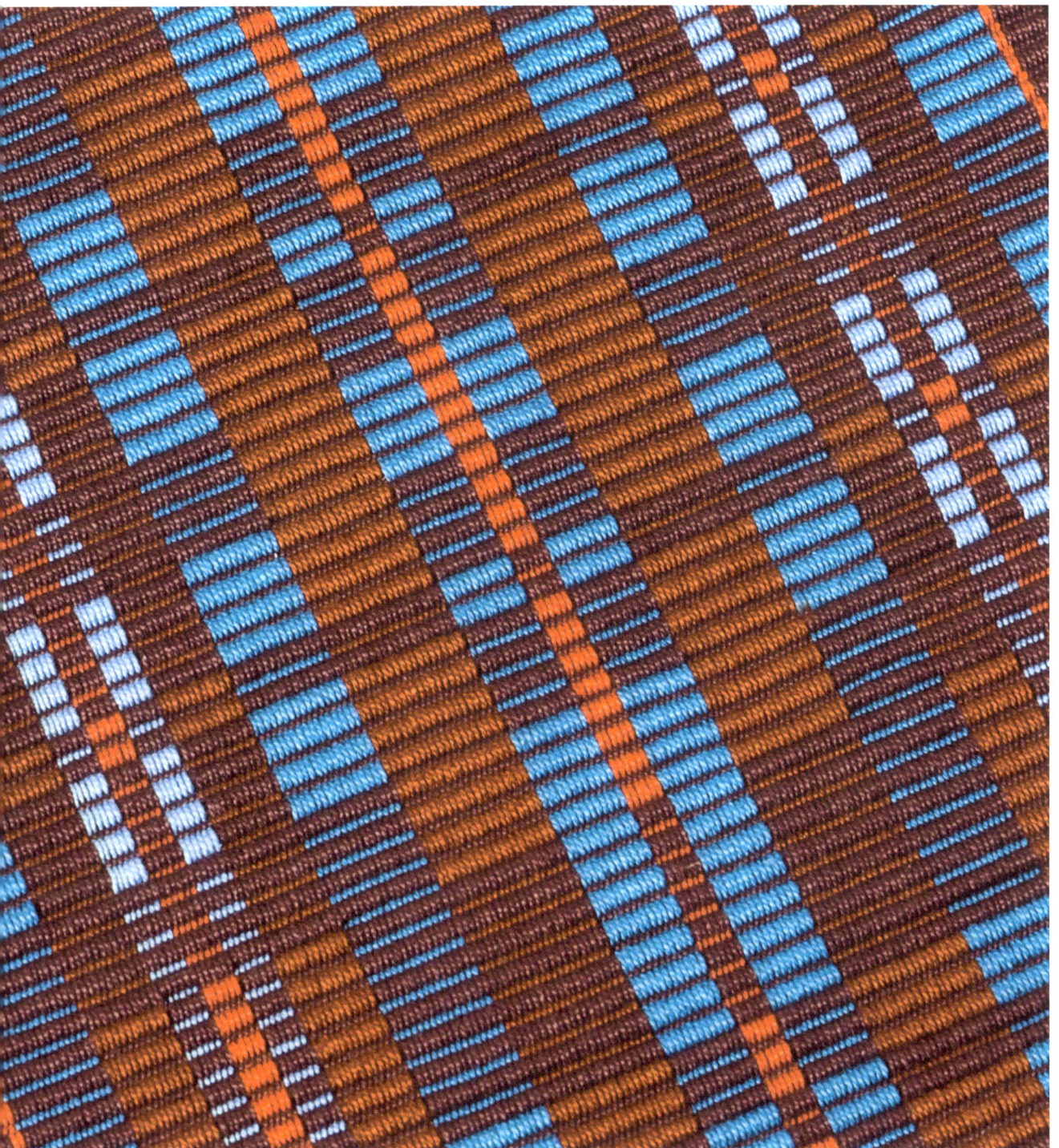

WEAVING

Start each placemat and the runner by weaving a hem. The treadling sequence shown here is for the table runner only. If you are making placemats, follow the treadling sequence on page 81.

TABLE MAT

Five Shades of Gray

This small mat, designed for a square table, offers an exercise in blending colors in the warp. The effect is best achieved with fine threads. To ensure better weft coverage, you'll make the warp with the double-thread method—a traditional Swedish technique.

MATERIALS

Finished dimensions: 12 in. x 17 in.

Warp	10/2 mercerized cotton, doubled (Lunatic Fringe): Black, Dark Gray, Medium Gray, Light Gray, Very Light Gray
Weft	
fine	10/2 mercerized cotton (Lunatic Fringe), Black
heavy	12 threads of 5/2 mercerized cotton (Lunatic Fringe), Black
Sett	40 epi
Reed	10 dents per inch
Sley	4 working ends (8 threads) per dent; thread 1 working end (2 threads) per heddle
Total ends	480 working ends
Width in reed	12 in.
Warp length	2 yd. *(loom waste included)*
Weft sett	8 ribs (heavy and fine) per 2 in.
Length on loom	20 in. *(under tension, hems included)*
Length off loom	19 in.
Finished length	17 in. *(washed, hemmed)*

MAKING THE WARP

The warp for this project is made using two fine threads as one working end. The working end is sleyed through the dent and is threaded in one heddle as if it were a single thread.

If you are dressing the loom from front to back, it is easier to make the warp in two separate chains: one for the top layer and one for the bottom layer. As you sley the reed, separate the two layers by running a heavy thread along the reed.

PROFILE DRAFT

				D				D			D		D				D				D
	C					C				C		C			C			C			
		B			B			B			B			B		B					
			A				A		A				A				A				
16	16	16	16	16	16	16	32	32	32	24	16	24	32	32	32	16	16	16	16	16	16

Working ends per block

WARP COLOR SEQUENCE

	20x	20x	20x	20x	20x	16x	8x	16x	20x	20x	20x	20x	20x	
480	2	2	2	2	2				2	2	2	2	2	● Black
48						1	2	1						○ Very Light Gray
152			1	2	1				1	2	1			○ Light Gray
160		1	2	1							1	2	1	◐ Medium Gray
120	2	1										1	2	● Dark Gray

960 threads/480 working ends

Because the warp threads in this project are fine, you'll use the Swedish double-thread method of making the warp—using two threads as one working end. For this project:

2 strands of 10/2 cotton = 1 working end

The two strands are not always the same color.

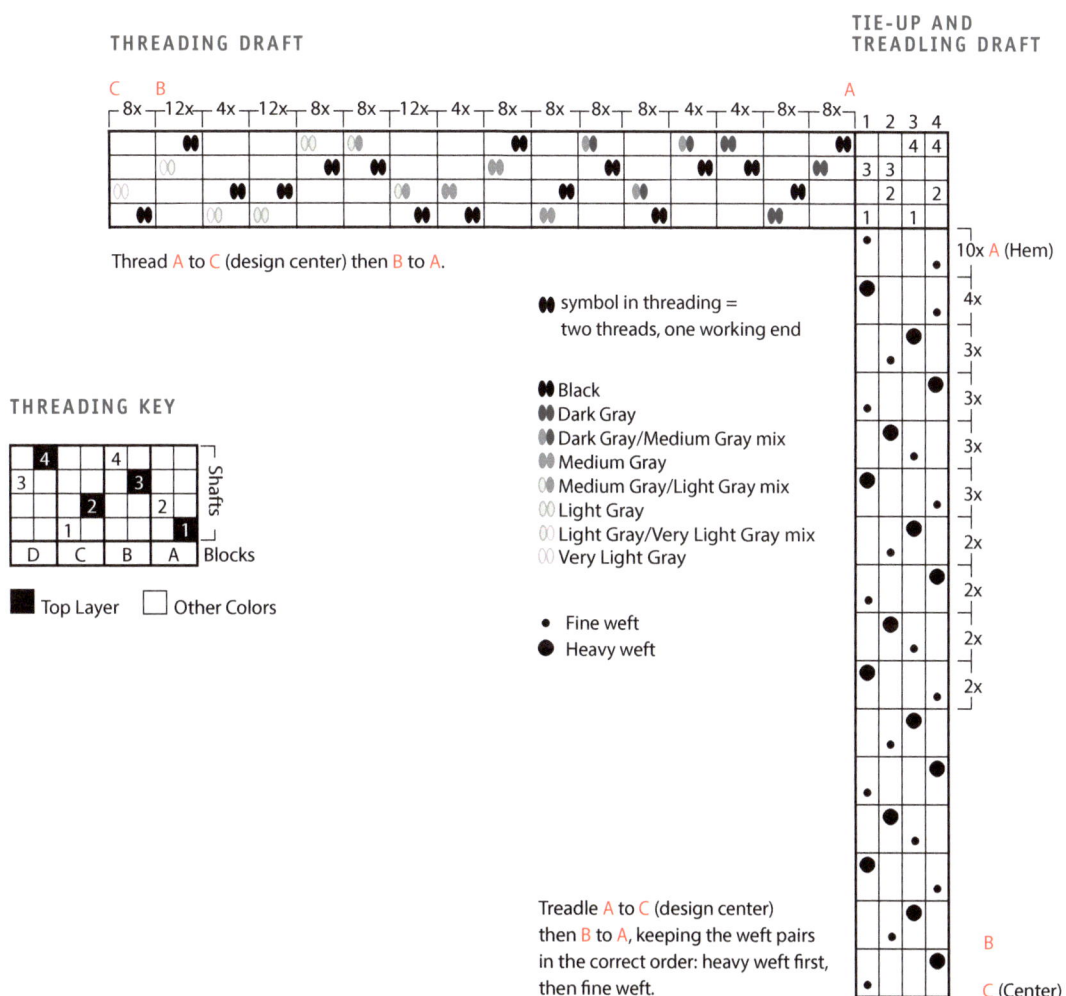

WEAVING

It's a good idea to sample the heavy weft before you begin, adding or subtracting threads to achieve the right weft thickness.

Start by weaving a fine hem and follow the treadling sequence. As you weave, be sure to square the blocks in the design whenever needed (see page 22).

EIGHT-SHAFT PROJECTS

Four-Block Patterns on Eight Shafts

WEAVING WITH EIGHT SHAFTS allows you the possibility of threading four independent blocks, which you may weave either singly or in combination with each other. In this section, I'll also introduce the skeleton tie-up, which makes it easier to treadle (see page 94–95).

The first project "Waiting for Summer" (page 92) presents weaving instructions for a pair of beach chair covers. I used 8/4 carpet warp for strength and durability. The blocks are used mostly in combination. The little border on each side adds another pattern repeat to this bold design.

The blocks in the table runner "Seven Shades of Reds" (page 97) are woven independently. I published this piece in *Handwoven* magazine almost thirty years ago. At the time I worked mainly with 6/2 unmercerized cotton, whose colors, unfortunately, fade over time. For this book, I wove the runner again, in 5/2 mercerized cotton and in different colors.

In the wall hanging "Undulations" (page 103), the blocks follow an undulating twill block design. The treadling follows the threading almost exactly, but with some reversals and different numbers of repeats. I've used this block design many times for placemats, bags, and boxes.

In the rug "Double Steps" (page 109), the blocks also follow each other but they are woven together—two blocks at a time in a continuous sequence (A and B, B and C, C and D, D and A, etc.). The warp is made with the double-thread method (see pages 88–89), which gives much more weight to the finished rug.

BEACH CHAIR COVERS

Waiting for Summer

These boldly patterned beach chair covers, woven with 8/4 carpet warp, are strong and durable. The first chair cover (at right) has a very long treadling sequence mostly because the side borders follow a set pattern. I simplified the border in the second chair cover design to shorten the treadling sequence.

MATERIALS

Finished dimensions: 18 in. x 42 in.

Warp		8/4 carpet warp (Maysville): Dark Navy Blue, Mahogany, Moody Blue, Oriental Beige
Weft		
	fine	10/2 mercerized cotton (UKI), Black
	heavy	11 threads of 8/4 carpet warp (Maysville), Dark Navy Blue
Sett		32 epi
Reed		8 dents per inch
Sley		4 ends per dent; thread 1 end per heddle
Total ends		576
Width in reed		18 in.
Warp length		5 yd. *(loom waste included)*
Weft sett		8 ribs (heavy and fine) per 2 in.
Length on loom		58 in. *(under tension, hems included)*
Length off loom		54 in.
Finished length		47.5 in. *(washed, hemmed)*

PROFILE DRAFT

	Border		Center		Border	
	D				D	
		C				
			B			
				A		
	64	56	336	56	64	Ends per block

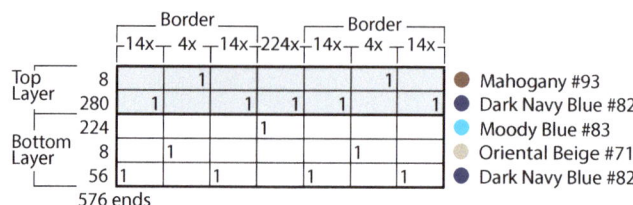

WARP COLOR SEQUENCE

- Mahogany #93
- Dark Navy Blue #82
- Moody Blue #83
- Oriental Beige #71
- Dark Navy Blue #82

WEAVING

Make a wide hem in order to accommodate the diameter of the wooden dowel that will hold the fabric on the chair frame. You may need to resize this part of the weaving (the header) according to your chair measurements. I used the skeleton tie-up, which allowed me to lift only two shafts at a time. This tie-up makes it easier to open the shed for the large center block (B). Follow the treadling sequence and end with another long hem. You'll weave the covers from seat to head rest.

The first chair cover I wove (Chair #1 in the draft, at right in the photo on page 93) had a long treadling sequence because the side borders follow a regular pattern. I simplified the border for the second chair to make the treadling more manageable.

The fabric was not washed. Even though I wove both chair covers to the same length and counted the same number of ribs, the fabric hung looser on the second chair. That's when I realized that the two chair frames were not exactly the same size. Measure each frame carefully before you begin.

SKELETON TIE-UP AND TREADLING DRAFT

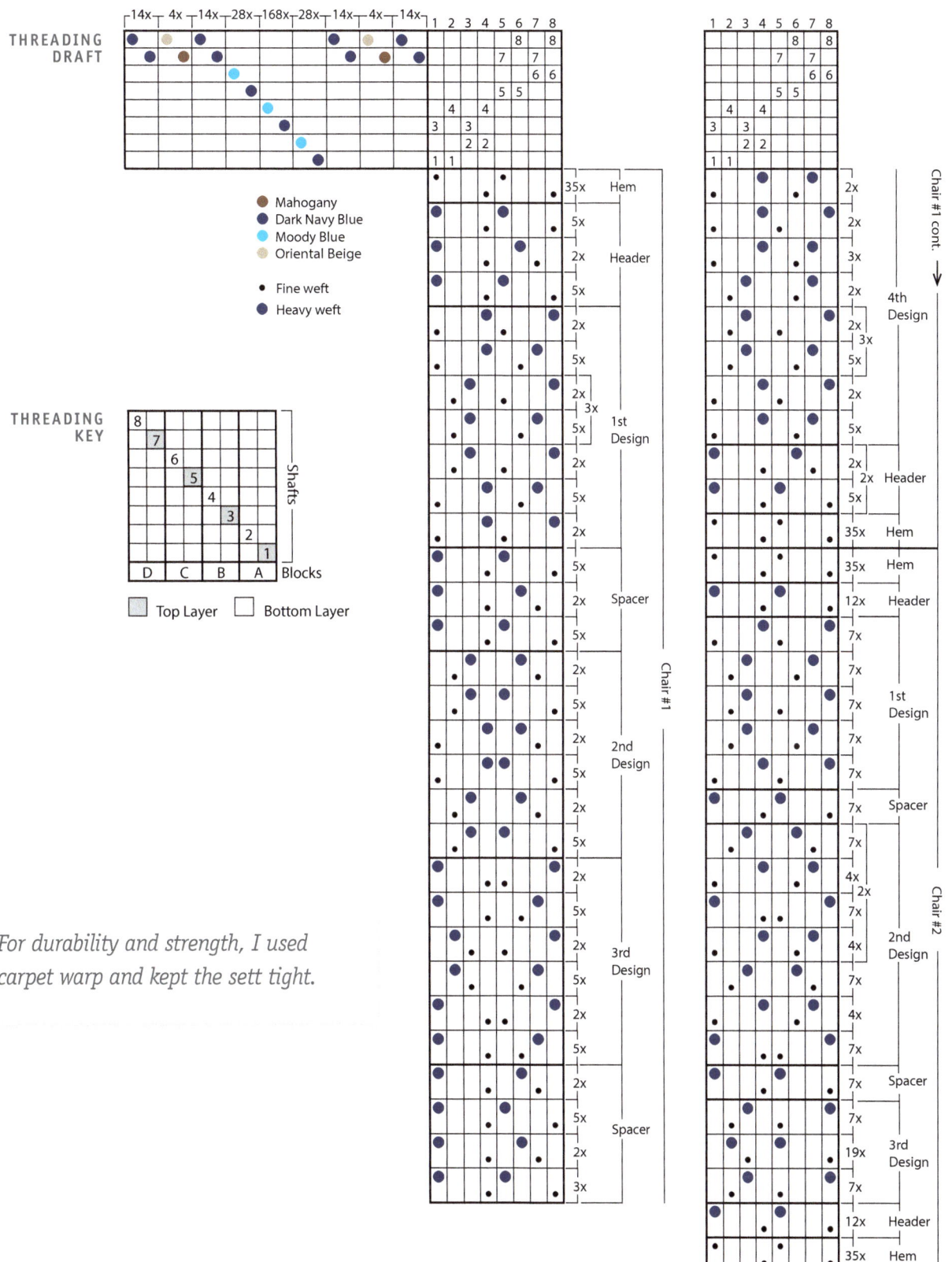

For durability and strength, I used carpet warp and kept the sett tight.

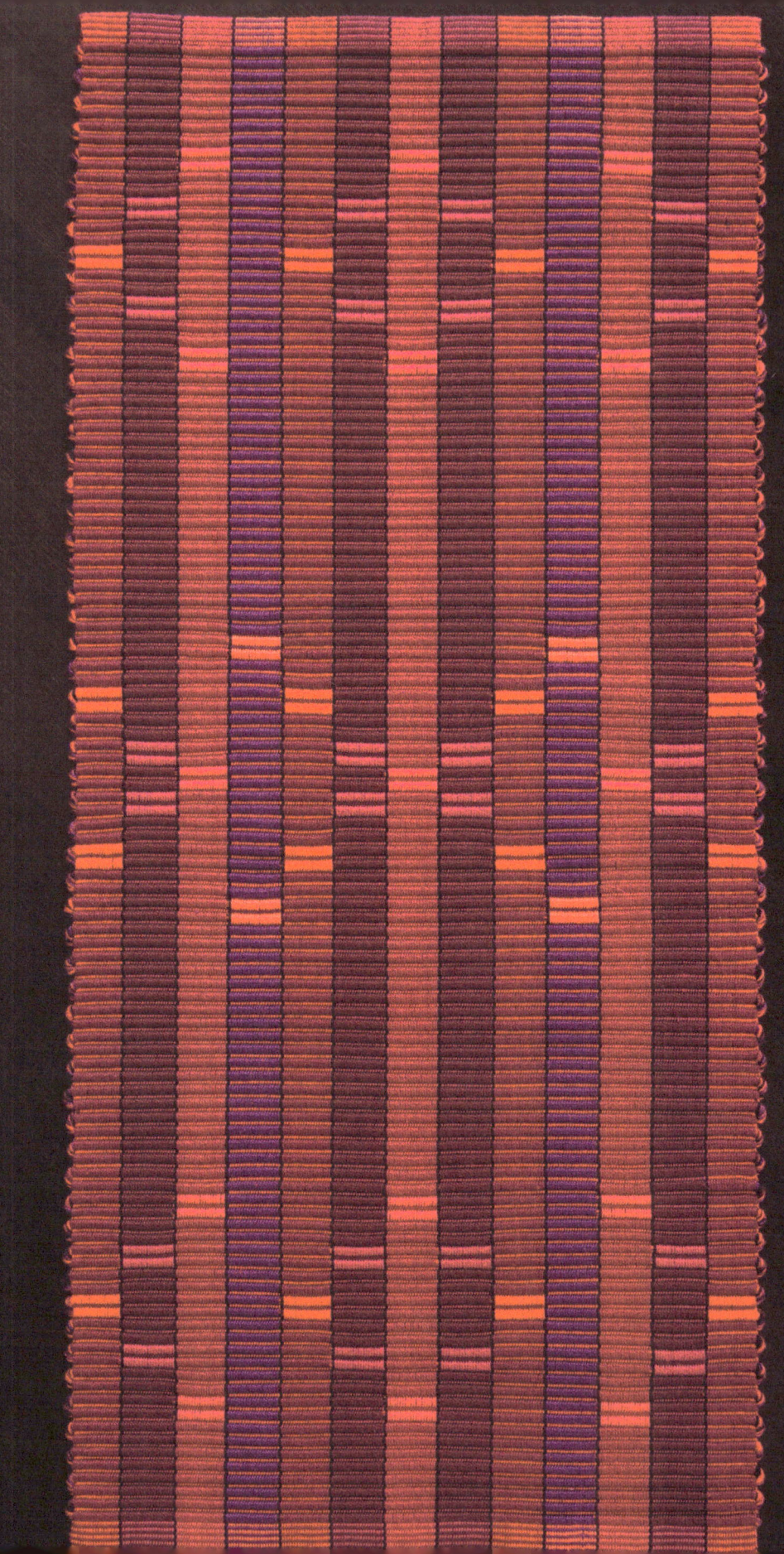

TABLE RUNNER

Seven Shades of Red

A thin line of solid black separates the blocks in this table runner. The blocks look best when they are woven independently. The heavy weft is a mix of red cotton threads, but it could also be black. Make the warp with as many colors as you wish or have.

MATERIALS

Finished dimensions: 13 in. x 28 in.

Warp	5/2 mercerized cotton (UKI): Wine, Maroon, Garnet, Wine Tone, Sangria, Fuchsia, Lipstick, Melon, Black
Weft	
fine	10/2 mercerized cotton (UKI), Black
heavy	12 threads of 5/2 mercerized cotton (UKI): mix of reds
Sett	40 epi
Reed	10 dents per inch
Sley	4 ends per dent; thread 1 end per heddle
Total ends	518
Width in reed	13 in.
Warp length	2 yd. *(loom waste included)*
Weft sett	8 ribs (heavy and fine) per 2 in.
Length on loom	34 in. *(under tension, hems included)*
Length off loom	32 in.
Finished length	28 in. *(washed, hemmed)*

REP RIPS REPS WEAVE

PROFILE DRAFT

			D				D					
		C			C			C				
	B			B		B			B			
A				A				A			A	
40	40	40	40	40	40	38	40	40	40	40	40	Ends per block

WARP COLOR SEQUENCE

C B → 19x → 19x → 19x → 19x → 19x → 19x A

Top Layer:
- 12 — Black #116
- 38 — Wine Tone #73
- 57 — Garnet #24
- 76 — Maroon #34
- 76 — Wine #17

Bottom Layer:
- 12 — Black #116
- 38 — Melon #107
- 57 — Lipstick #32
- 76 — Fuchsia #3
- 76 — Sangria #130

518 total ends

Warp A to C then B to A.

THREADING DRAFT

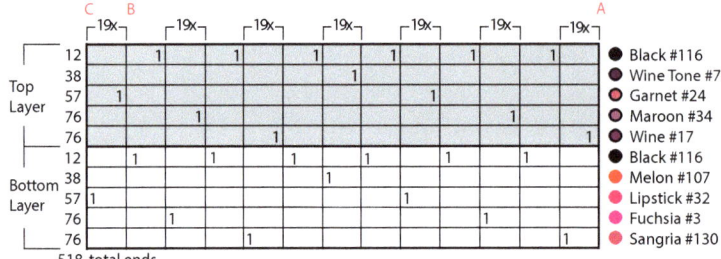

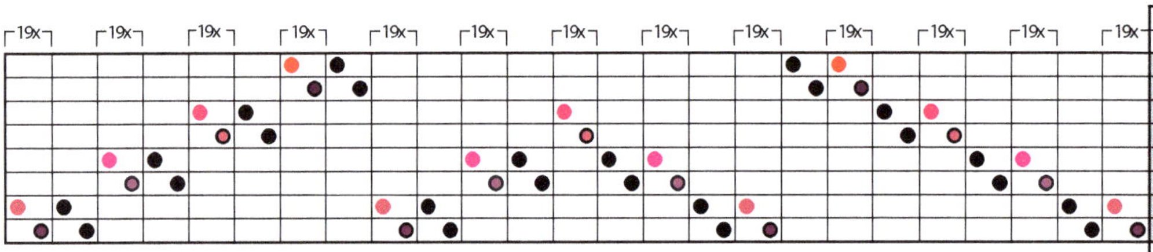

TRADITIONAL TIE-UP AND TREADLING DRAFT

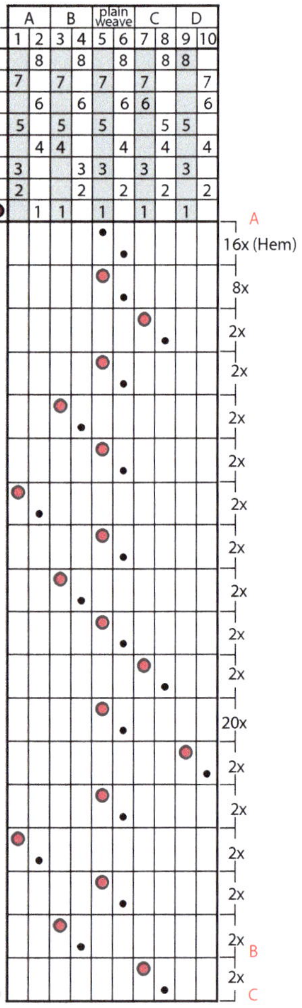

Note: Shaded treadles are for heavy weft.

THREADING KEY

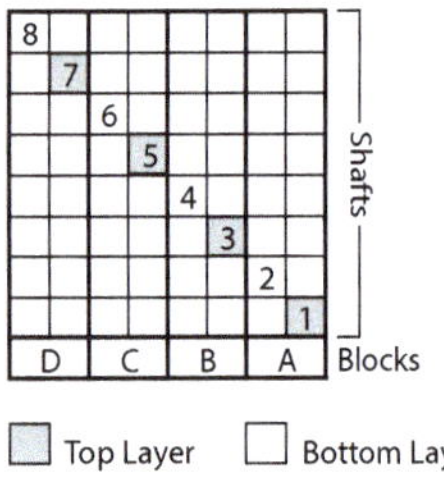

Shafts 1–8, Blocks D C B A

- Top Layer (shaded)
- Bottom Layer

Colors:
- Black
- Wine Tone
- Garnet
- Maroon
- Wine
- Black
- Melon
- Lipstick
- Fuchsia
- Sangria

- • Fine weft
- ● Heavy weft

Treadle A to C (design center) then from B to A, keeping the weft pairs in the correct order: heavy weft first, then fine weft.

(Center)

REVERSE SIDE >

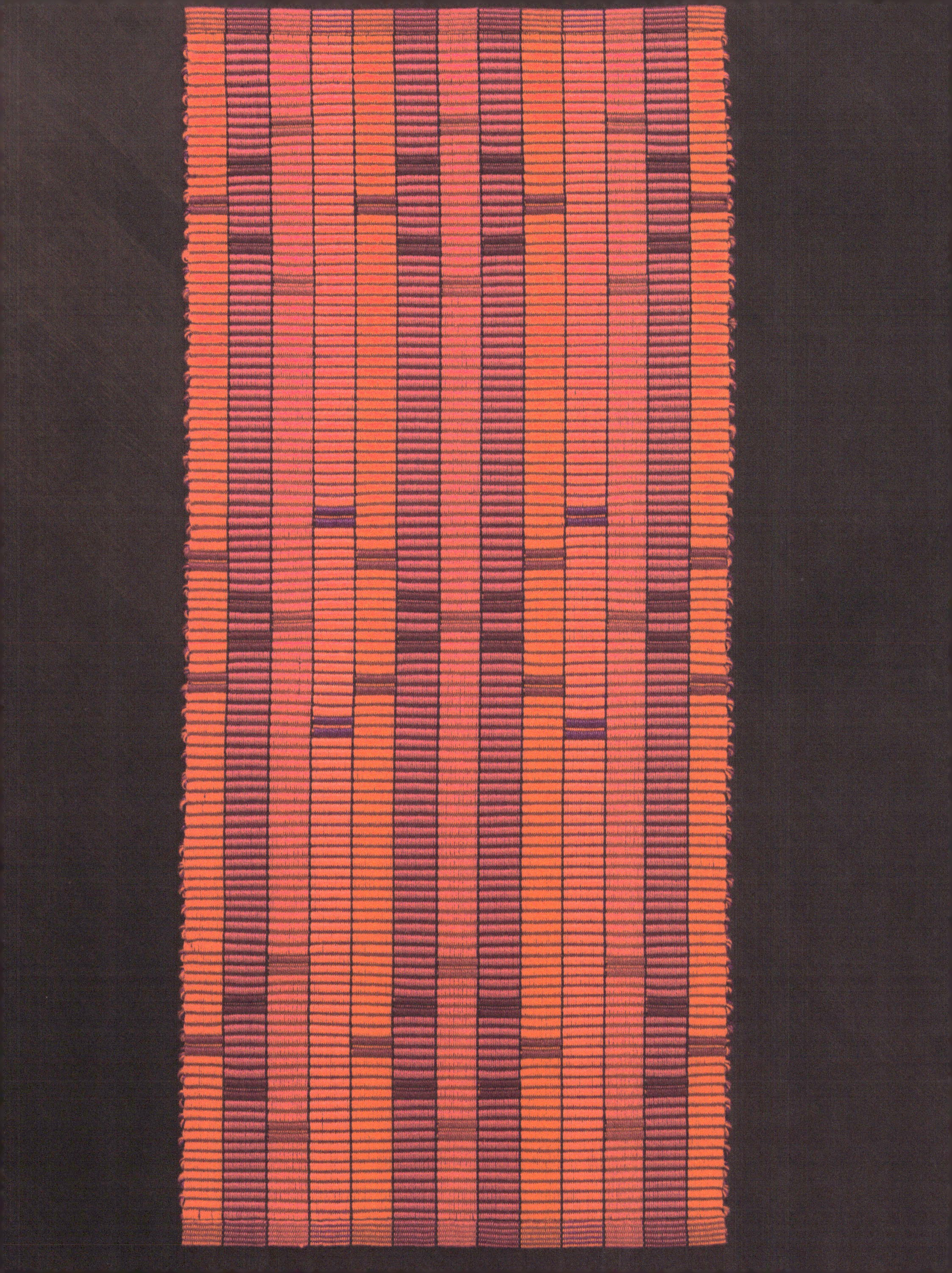

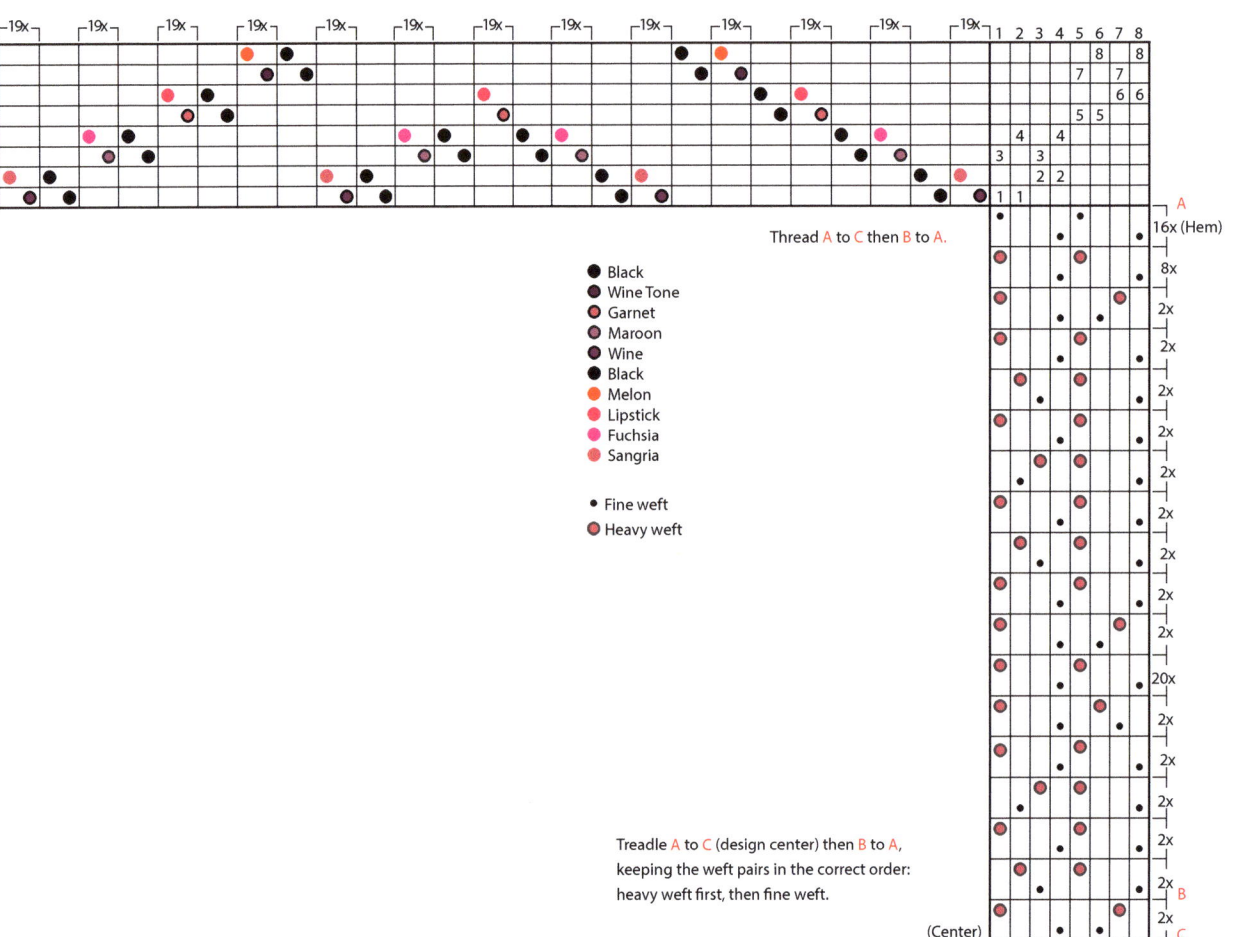

WEAVING

Start by weaving a fine hem. Then follow the treadling sequence. The blocks in this runner are woven independently. I have provided two tie-ups, so you have a choice of a traditional tie-up or a skeleton tie-up. With the skeleton tie-up, you treadle with both feet at the same time, which opens the shed more easily.

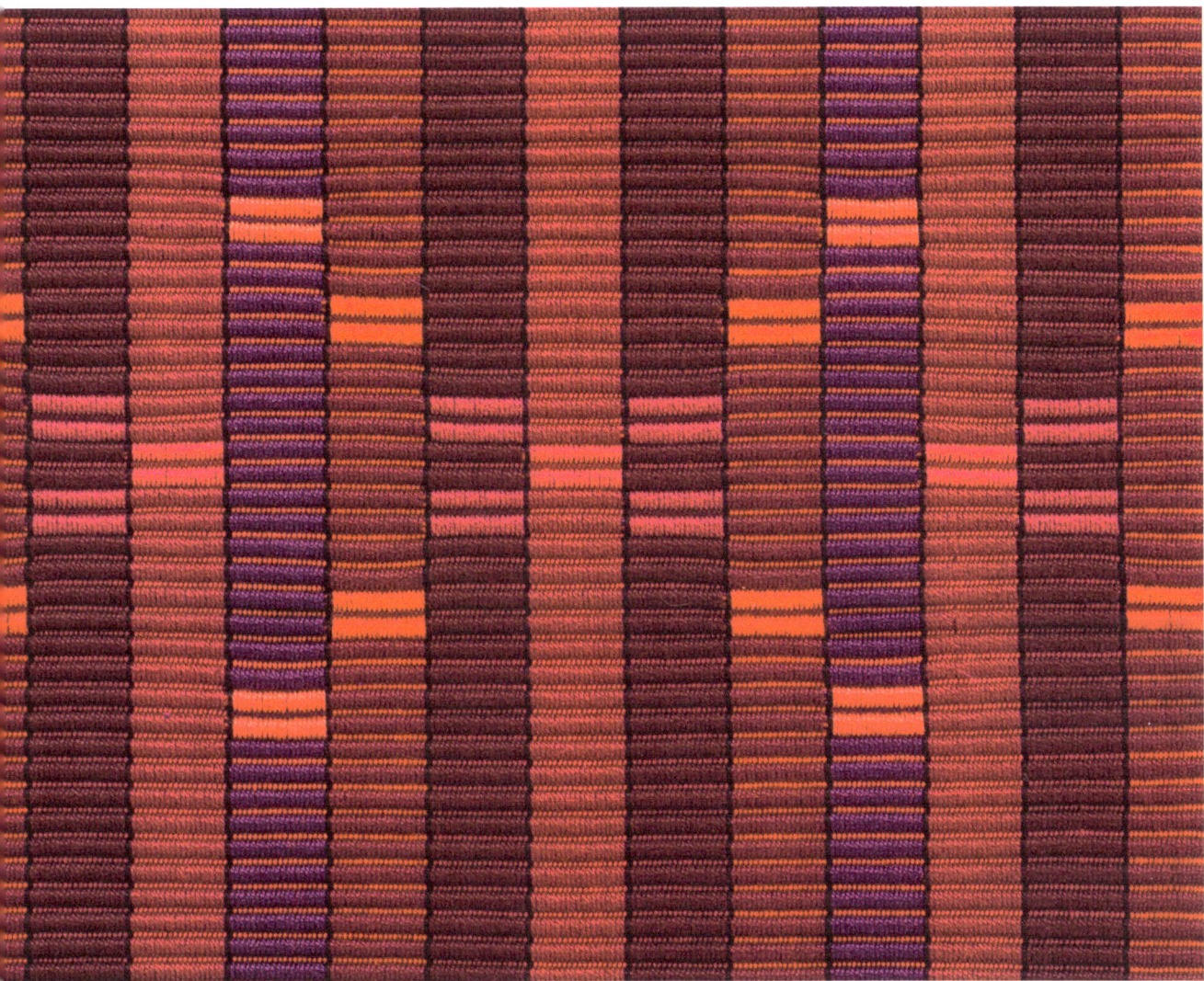

SKELETON TIE-UP

To make the treadling easier, I prefer the skeleton tie-up. With a skeleton tie-up you are lifting only two shafts at a time. The weaving is much easier—and you won't need to go under the loom to change the tie-up while you're weaving.

The skeleton tie-up on eight shafts allows sixteen possible treadling combinations.

1	2	3	4	5	6	7	8	Treadle #
					8		8	
				7		7		
						6	6	
				5	5			
	4		4					
3		3						
		2	2					
1	1							
Left foot				Right foot				

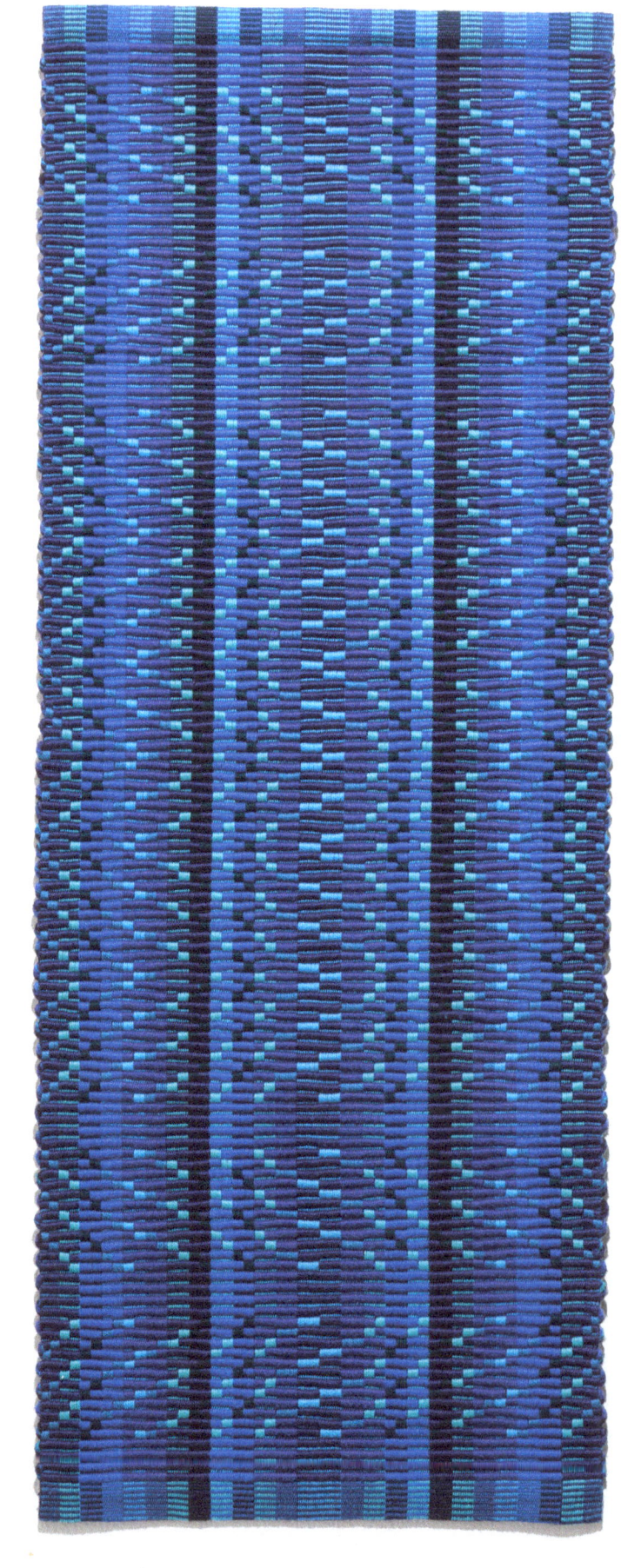

WALL HANGING

Undulations

I weave this undulating twill block sequence quite often. The flow of the design shows best in a wall hanging, but it also works well for placemats and for bags and boxes (see pages 158–162).

MATERIALS

Finished dimensions: 13 in. x 30 in.

Warp	5/2 mercerized cotton (UKI): Cobalt Blue, Yale Blue, Navy, Bermuda Blue, Forest, Duck, Quarry
Weft	
fine	10/2 mercerized cotton (UKI), Black
heavy	12 threads of 5/2 mercerized cotton (UKI): mix of dark blues
Sett	40 epi
Reed	10 dents per inch
Sley	4 ends per dent; thread 1 end per heddle
Total ends	520
Width in reed	13 in.
Warp length	3 yd. *(loom waste included)*
Weft sett	9 ribs (heavy and fine) per 2 in.
Length on loom	40 in. *(under tension, hems included)*
Length off loom	37 in.
Finished length	33 in. *(hemmed)*

PROFILE DRAFT

D				D				D				D				D			
	C				C				C				C				C		
		B				B				B				B				B	
			A				A				A				A				A
20	20	10	10	10	10	10	10	10	20	20	20	20	10	10	10	10	10	10	10

← cont'd.

D				D				D				D				D				
	C				C				C				C				C			
		B				B				B				B				B		
			A				A				A				A				A	
10	10	10	10	10	10	10	20	20	20	20	10	10	10	10	10	10	10	20	20	Ends per block

WARP COLOR SEQUENCE

		C 10x	20x	10x	B 10x	10x	10x	10x	10x	10x	10x	10x	10x	10x	10x A	
Top Layer	80	1		1	1					1	1					Cobalt Blue #75
	80					1	1					1	1			Yale Blue #63
	100		1					1	1					1	1	Navy #15
Bottom Layer	40		1								1					Bermuda Blue #109
	60					1		1					1			Forest #137
	80				1		1		1					1		Duck #60
	80	1		1						1		1			1	Quarry #147

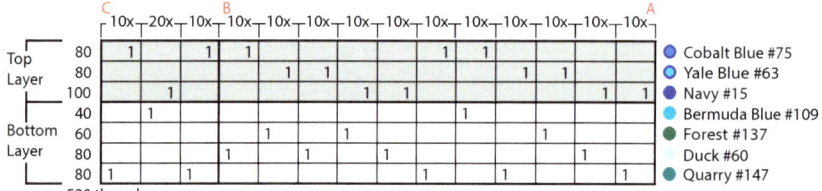

520 threads

Warp A to C then B to A.

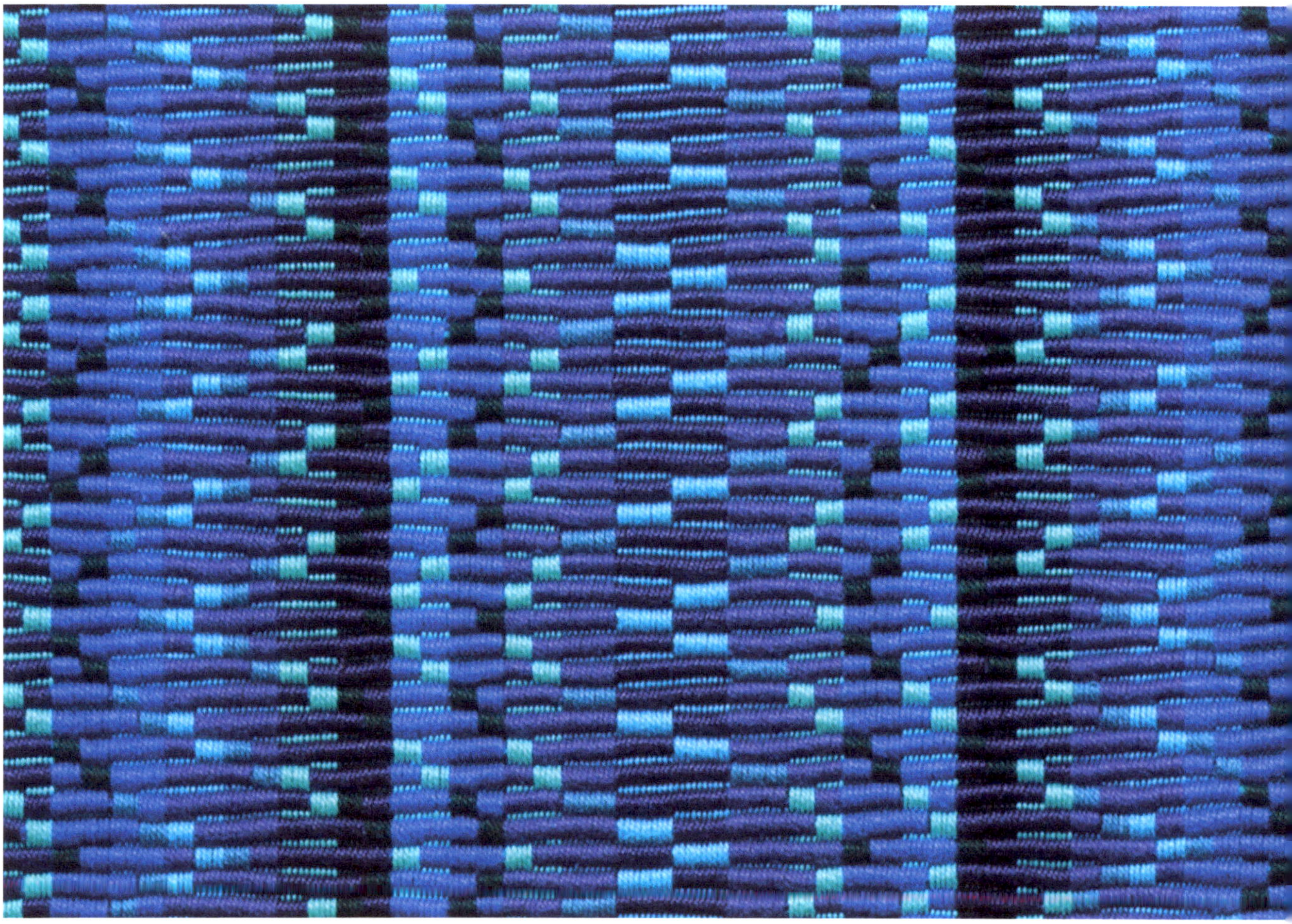

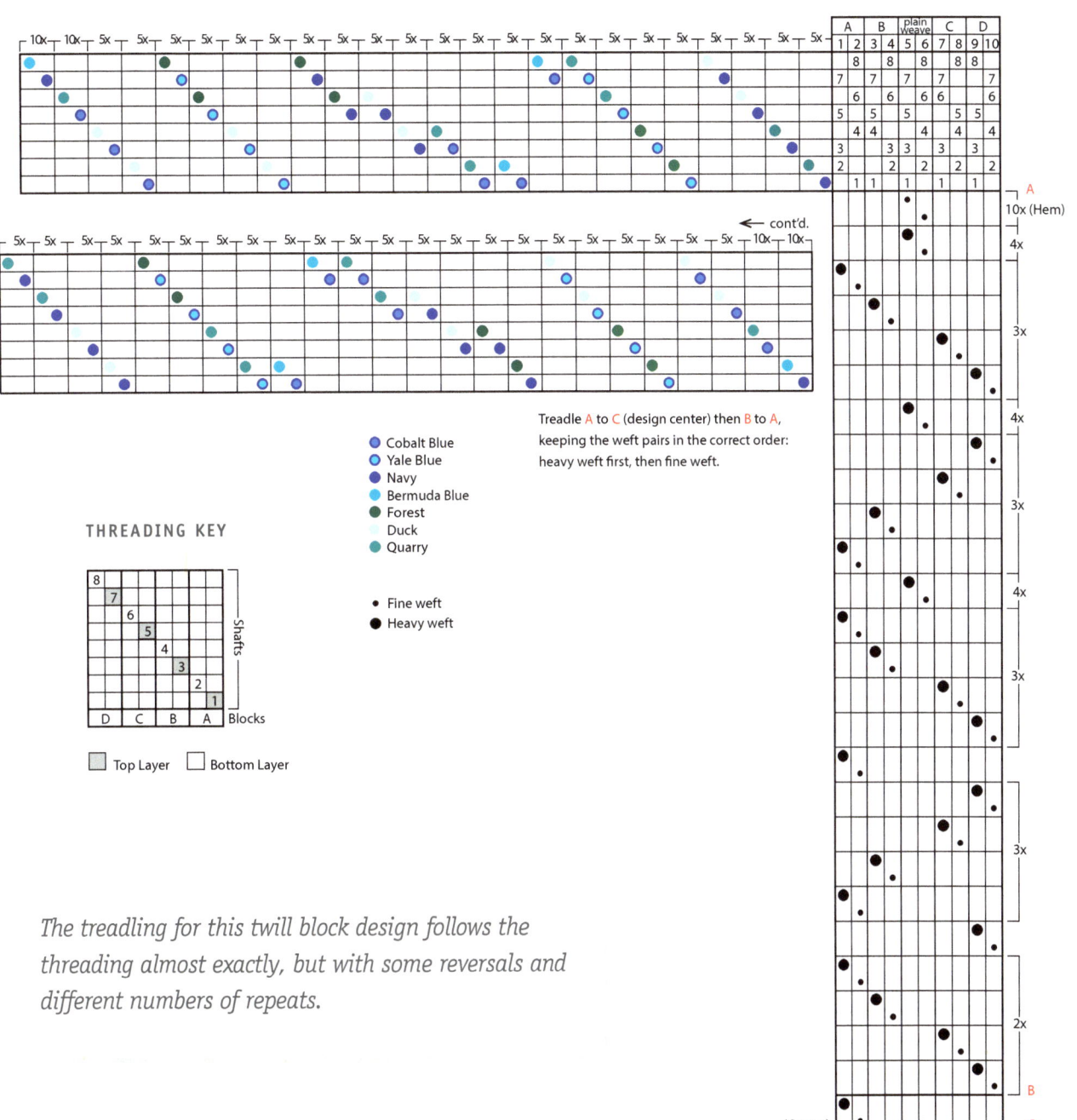

WEAVING

With the fine weft, weave a hem long enough to accommodate the diameter of a dowel or other hanging device. Follow the treadling sequence, paying attention to the many repeats and keeping track of the direction of the treadling.

You will weave the pattern blocks singly so I am providing both the traditional and skeleton tie-ups (see page 101).

EIGHT-SHAFT PROJECTS 105

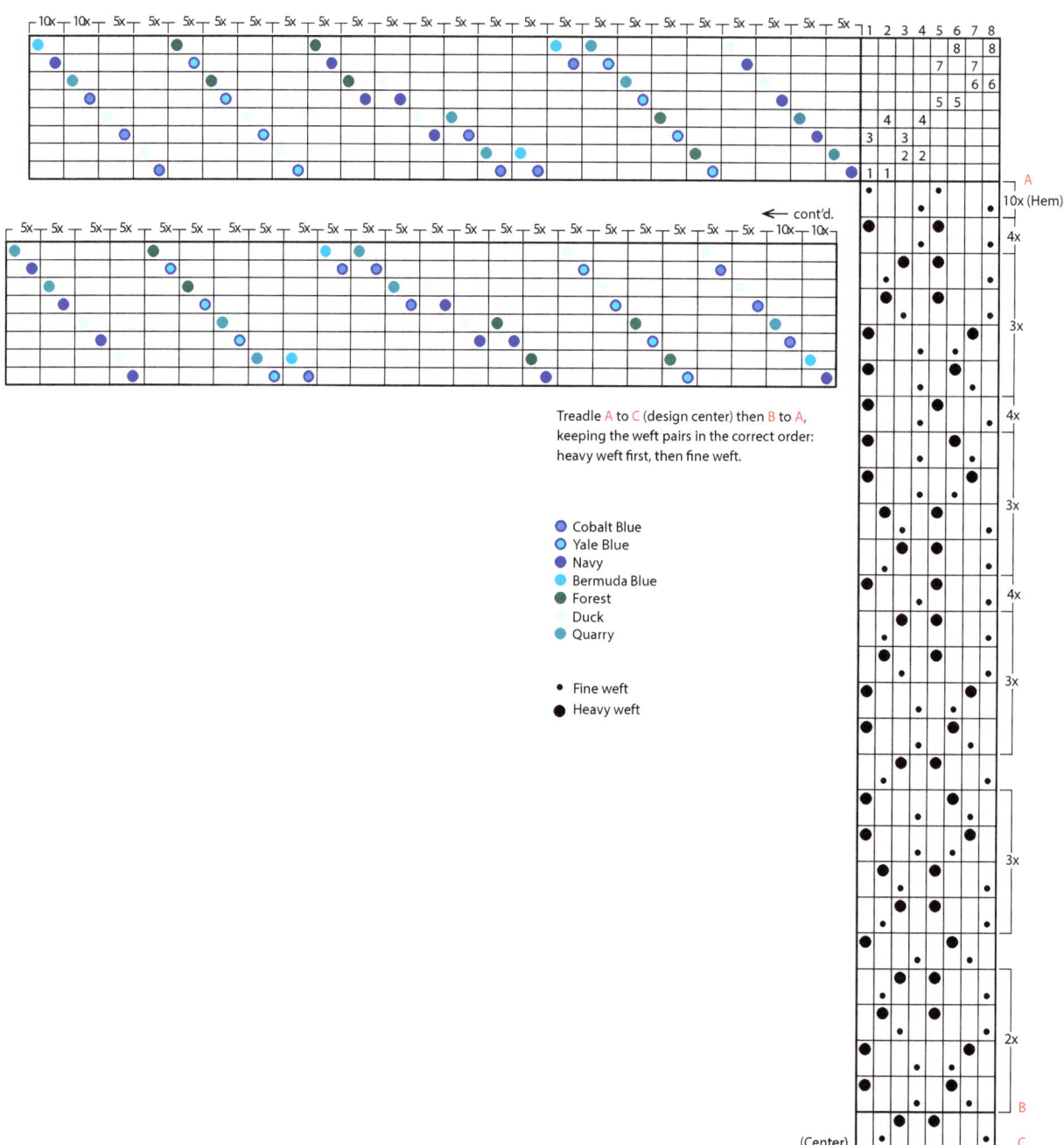

WEAVING

With the fine weft, weave a hem long enough to accommodate the diameter of a dowel or other hanging device. Follow the treadling sequence, paying attention to the many repeats and keeping track of the direction of the treadling.

You will weave the pattern blocks singly so I am providing both the traditional and skeleton tie-ups (see page 101).

RUG

Double Steps

The warp for this rug is made with the double-thread method—two threads combine to make one working end. The double-thread warp gives extra weight to the rug, and a hard beat will keep the rug lying flat on the floor.

MATERIALS

Finished dimensions: 23 in. x 51 in.

Warp	5/2 mercerized cotton (UKI): Medium Brown, Dark Sierra, Mead, Old Gold, Chamois, Champagne, Natural
Weft	
fine	10/2 mercerized cotton (UKI), Black
heavy	14 threads of 5/2 mercerized cotton (UKI): mix of browns
Sett	24 epi
Reed	12 dents per inch
Sley	2 working ends (4 threads) per dent; thread 1 working end (2 threads) per heddle
Total ends	570 working ends
Width in reed	23.75 in.
Warp length	3.25 yd. *(loom waste included)*
Weft sett	9 ribs (heavy and fine) per 2 in.
Length on loom	57 in. *(under tension, hems included)*
Length off loom	54 in.
Finished length	51 in. *(hemmed)*

EIGHT-SHAFT PROJECTS

MAKING THE WARP

This warp is made the Swedish way, using two threads together as one working end (see pages 88–89). Sometimes the two threads are different colors. The double-thread working end is sleyed through the dent and is threaded in one heddle.

When dressing the loom from front to back, it is easier to make the warp in two separate chains—especially when working with so many color changes. Make a chain for the top layer and one for the bottom layer. As you sley the reed, separate the two layers with a heavy thread running along the reed.

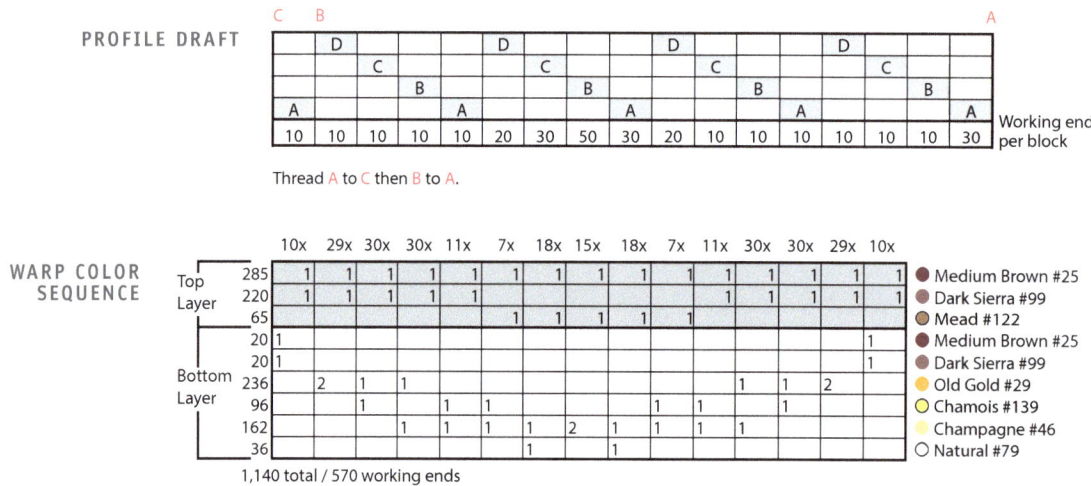

PROFILE DRAFT

Thread A to C then B to A.

WARP COLOR SEQUENCE

1,140 total / 570 working ends

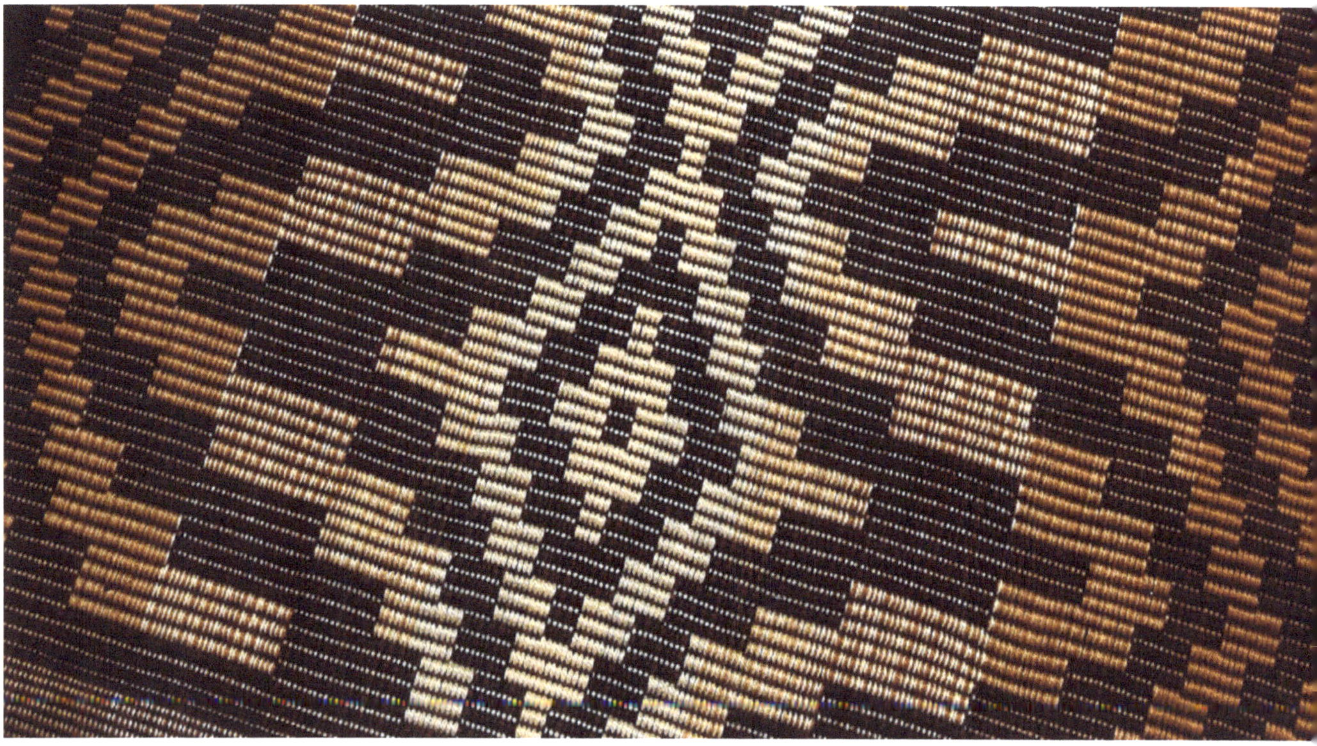

- Medium Brown #25
- Dark Sierra #99
- Mead #122
- Medium Brown #25
- Dark Sierra #99
- Old Gold #29
- Chamois #139
- Champagne #46
- Natural #79

THREADING DRAFT

SKELETON TIE-UP AND TREADLING DRAFT

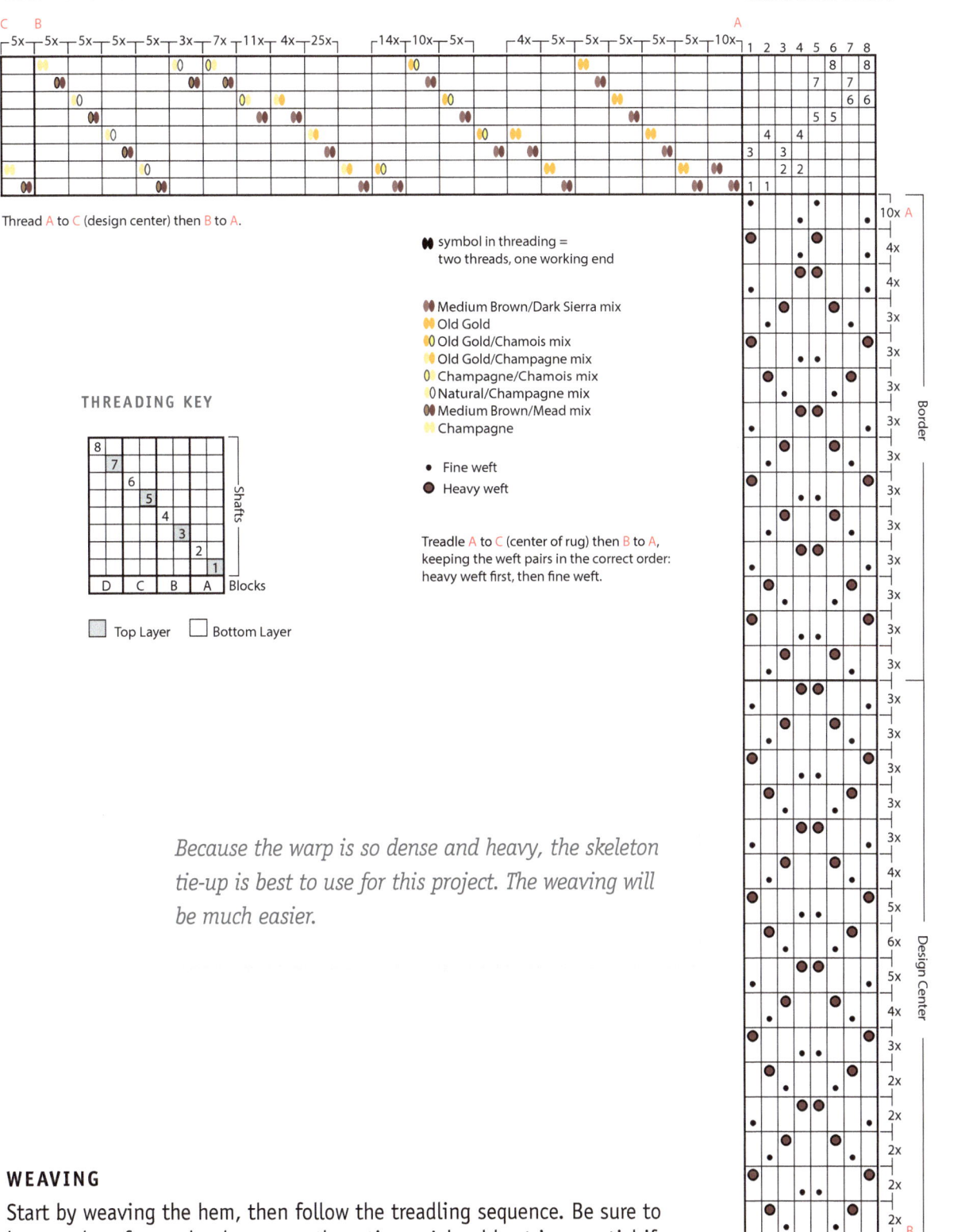

Thread A to C (design center) then B to A.

● symbol in threading =
two threads, one working end

● Medium Brown/Dark Sierra mix
● Old Gold
● Old Gold/Chamois mix
● Old Gold/Champagne mix
● Champagne/Chamois mix
● Natural/Champagne mix
● Medium Brown/Mead mix
● Champagne

• Fine weft
● Heavy weft

Treadle A to C (center of rug) then B to A, keeping the weft pairs in the correct order: heavy weft first, then fine weft.

THREADING KEY

Top Layer Bottom Layer

Because the warp is so dense and heavy, the skeleton tie-up is best to use for this project. The weaving will be much easier.

WEAVING

Start by weaving the hem, then follow the treadling sequence. Be sure to beat each weft very hard—two or three times. A hard beat is essential if you want the rug to lie flat on the floor.

EIGHT-SHAFT PROJECTS

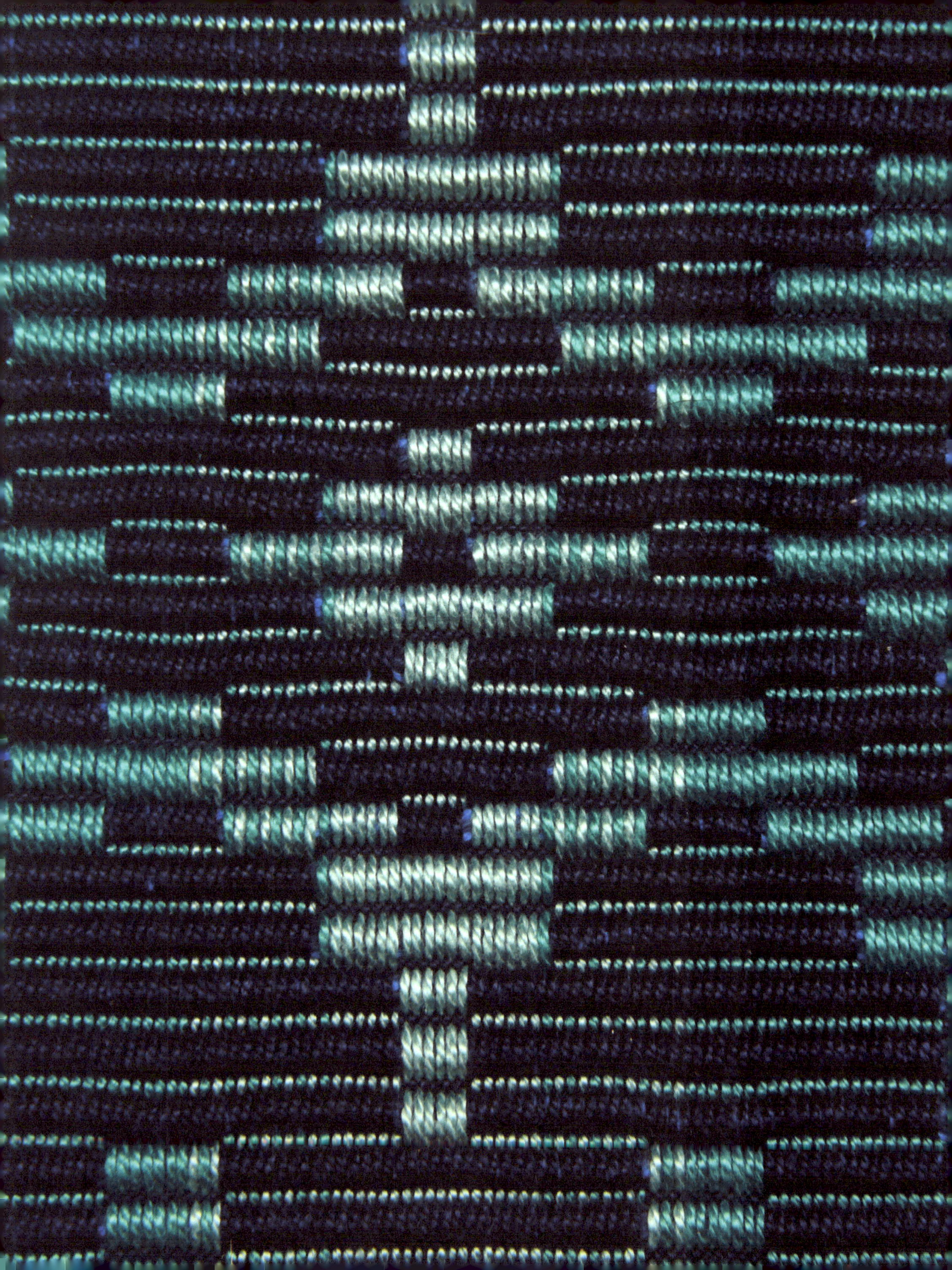

Eight-Block Patterns on Eight Shafts

WHEN YOU WEAVE WITH EIGHT SHAFTS and draft eight blocks, you greatly increase the number of design possibilities. The first four blocks (A, B, C, D) are threaded on separate pairs of adjacent shafts. The next four blocks (E, F, G, H) will use the same shafts in the reverse order. Every shed opening will consist of four pattern and four background blocks.

There are sixteen block combinations possible with eight blocks and eight shafts—but we will not use them all.

The blocks in the first project, "Reflections" (page 115), a three-panel wall hanging, are mirror images vertically. You can use the same draft to weave placemats and table runners if you wish.

The second project, "Sitting Pretty" (page 121), is a bench cushion with large design areas that contrast with the background. The cushion is not bulky, and the plain-weave section of the fabric makes a good lining for finishing the underside.

"Diamonds, Owl, Clown, and Butterfly" (page 125) are designs from a longer sampler that I always propose my workshop students make. These blocks are the most popular patterns—and they are good examples of eight-block, eight-shaft designs. I have presented only a few of the treadling sequences that are possible, but I hope you will be inspired to experiment on your own.

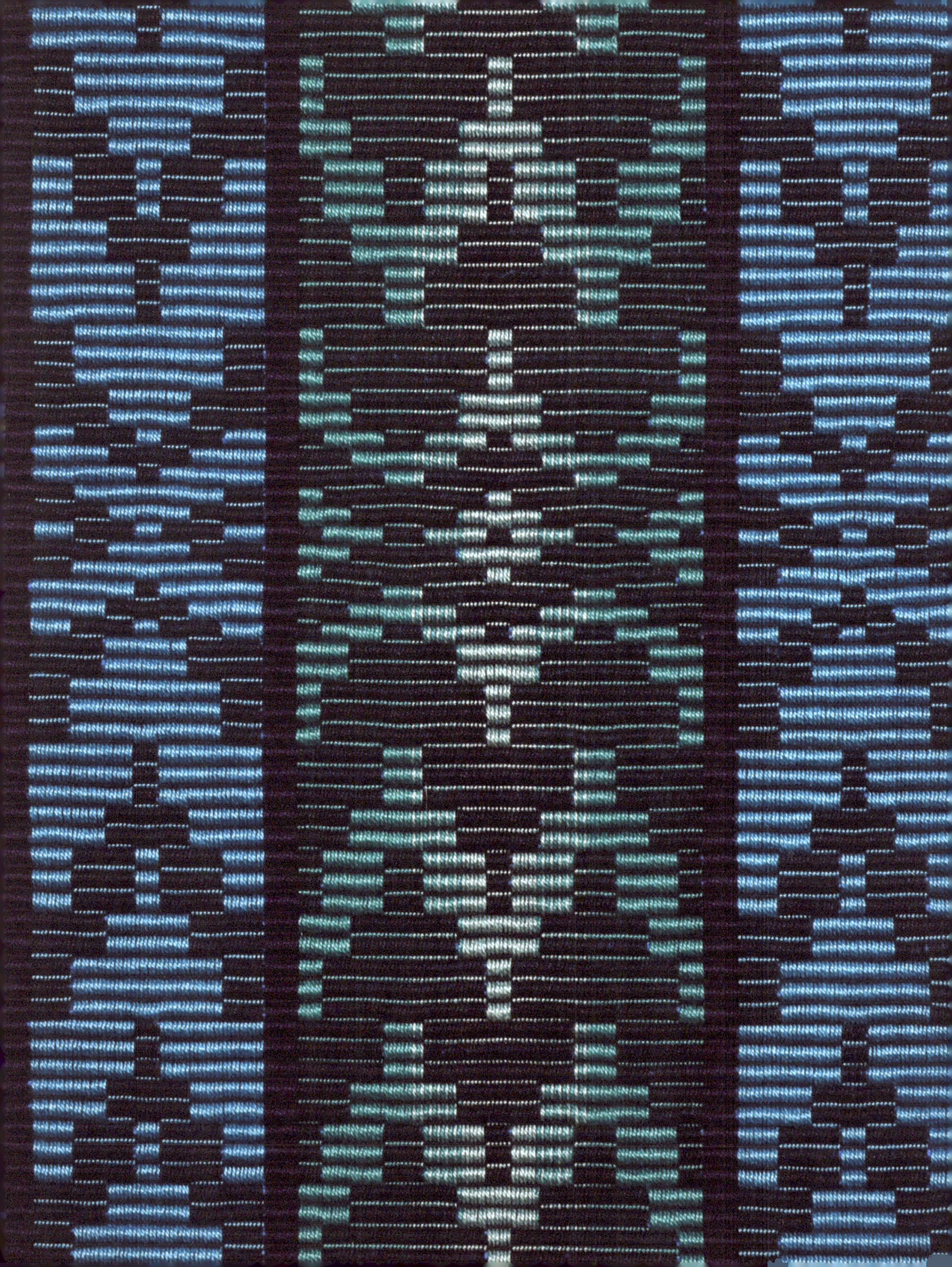

WALL HANGING

Reflections

The block patterns in this three-panel wall hanging are mirror images vertically. You can also make placemats and table runners with the same design. The rectangular panel is shown on the facing page. All three panels are shown on pages 116–117.

MATERIALS

Finished dimensions: square panels 12 in. x 13 in.; rectangular panel 12 in. x 20 in.

Warp	5/2 mercerized cotton (UKI): Navy, Jade Green, Deep Purple, Duck, Special Turq
Weft	
fine	10/2 mercerized cotton (UKI), Black
heavy	11 threads of 5/2 mercerized cotton (UKI), Navy
Sett	40 epi
Reed	10 dents per inch
Sley	1 end per dent; thread 1 end per heddle
Total ends	484
Width in reed	12 in.
Warp length	3 yd. *(loom waste included)*
Weft sett	8 ribs (heavy and fine) per 2 in.
Length on loom	square panels 16.5 in.; rectangular panel 24 in. *(under tension, hems included)*
Length off loom	square panels 14.5 in.; rectangular panel 22 in.
Finished length	square panels 13 in.; rectangular panel 20 in. *(hemmed)*

EIGHT-SHAFT PROJECTS

116 REP RIPS REPS WEAVE

EIGHT-SHAFT PROJECTS 117

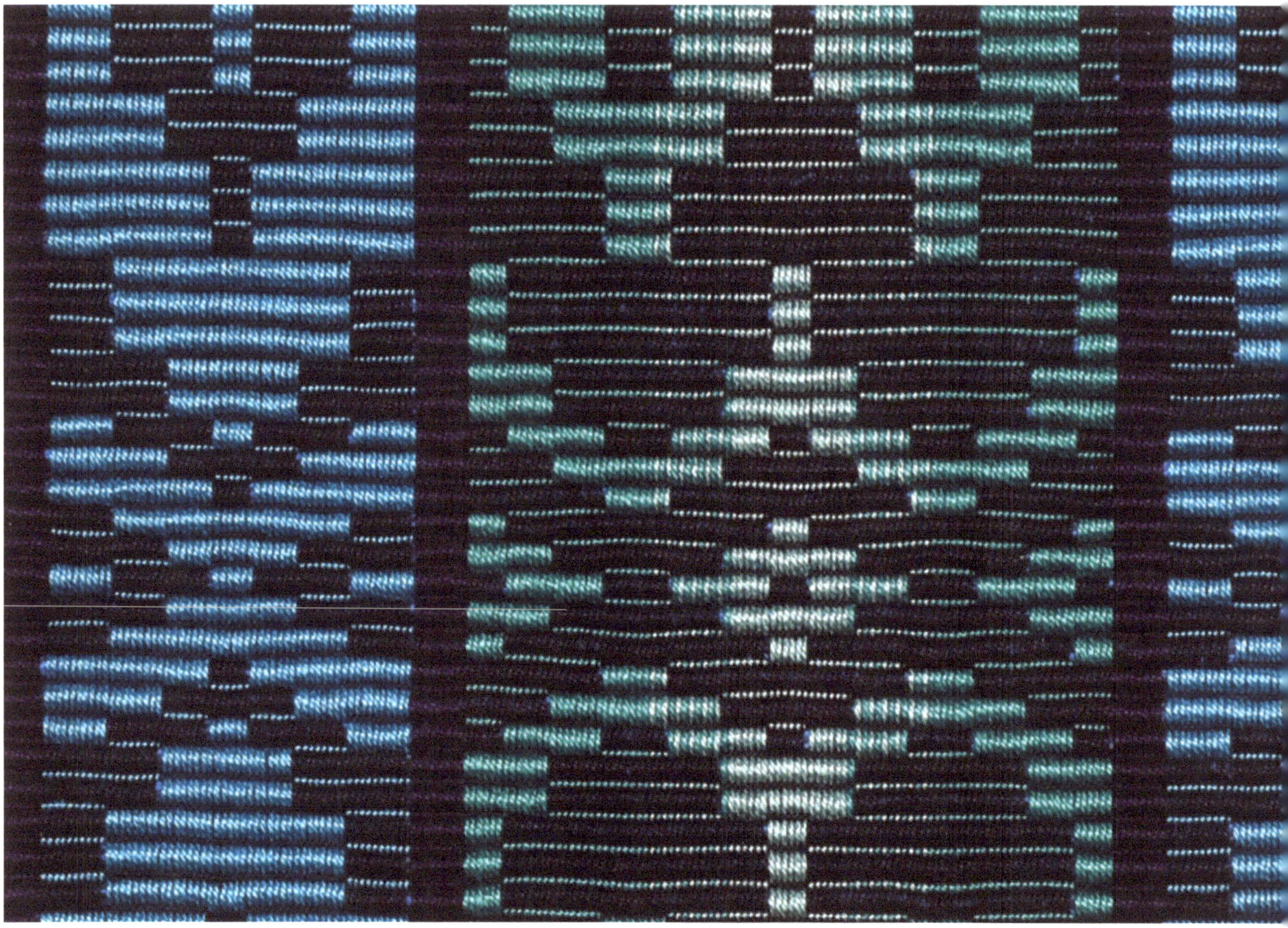

PROFILE DRAFT

C	B														A	
H					H											
	G			G												
		F	F													
		E														
								D					D			
							C				C					
						B		B								
					A					A				A		
12	14	16	20	16	14	12	16	20	16	14	12	14	16	20	16	Ends per block

Thread A to C then B to A.

WARP COLOR SEQUENCE

	C	B	18x	6x	28x	8x	56x	8x	A	
Top Layer	16							1		● Deep Purple #120
	226		1	1	1	1	1			● Navy #15
	30	1		1						Duck #60
Bottom Layer	68		1		1					● Jade Green #135
	112						1			● Special Turq #44
	16					1				● Deep Purple #120
	16						1			● Navy #15

484 threads

Warp A to C then B to A.

WEAVING

Start all three panels with generous hems to allow for the diameter of the dowels or other hanging devices. Because the pieces are not entirely symmetrical—the top is slightly different from the bottom—the treadling sequences are long.

Carefully record your measurements as you weave—counting ribs and measuring with a tape measure—to be sure the two square panels are the same size.

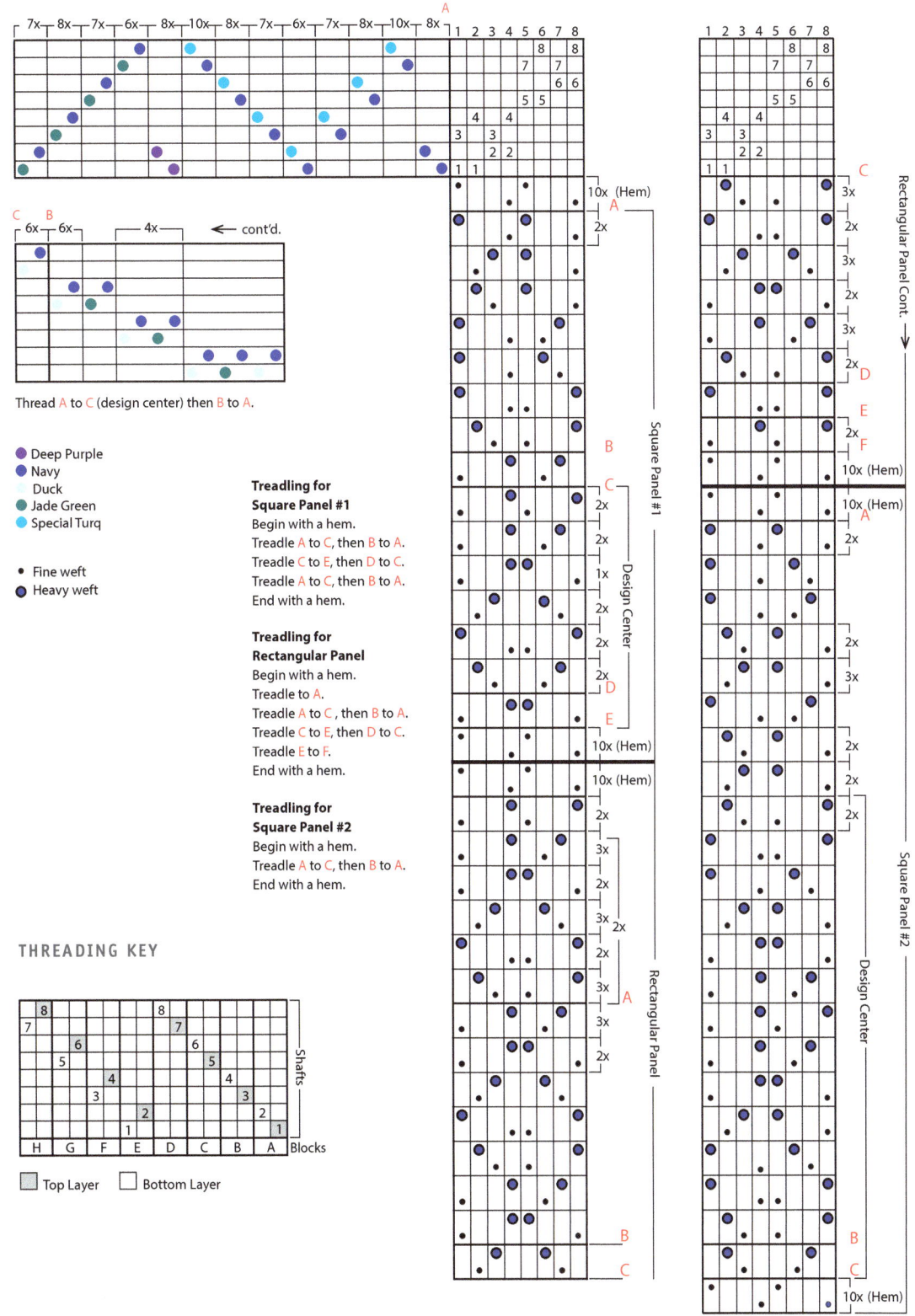

EIGHT-SHAFT PROJECTS 119

BENCH CUSHION

Sitting Pretty

I always wanted to make a small cushion for my loom bench. This one is not bulky, and an additional plain-weave length of fabric makes a good lining for the underside.

MATERIALS

Finished dimensions: 11 in. x 22 in.

Warp	5/2 mercerized cotton (UKI): Quarry, Dark Sierra, Burnt Orange, Light Rust
Weft	
fine	10/2 mercerized cotton (UKI), Black
heavy	10 threads of 5/2 mercerized cotton (UKI), Quarry
Sett	40 epi
Reed	10 dents per inch
Sley	4 ends per dent; thread 1 end per heddle
Total ends	444
Width in reed	11 in.
Warp length	2.5 yd. *(loom waste included)*
Weft sett	9 ribs (heavy and fine) per 2 in.
Length on loom	44 in. *(under tension, lining and hems included)*
Length off loom	42 in.
Finished length	19.5 in. *(washed, lined, and hemmed)*

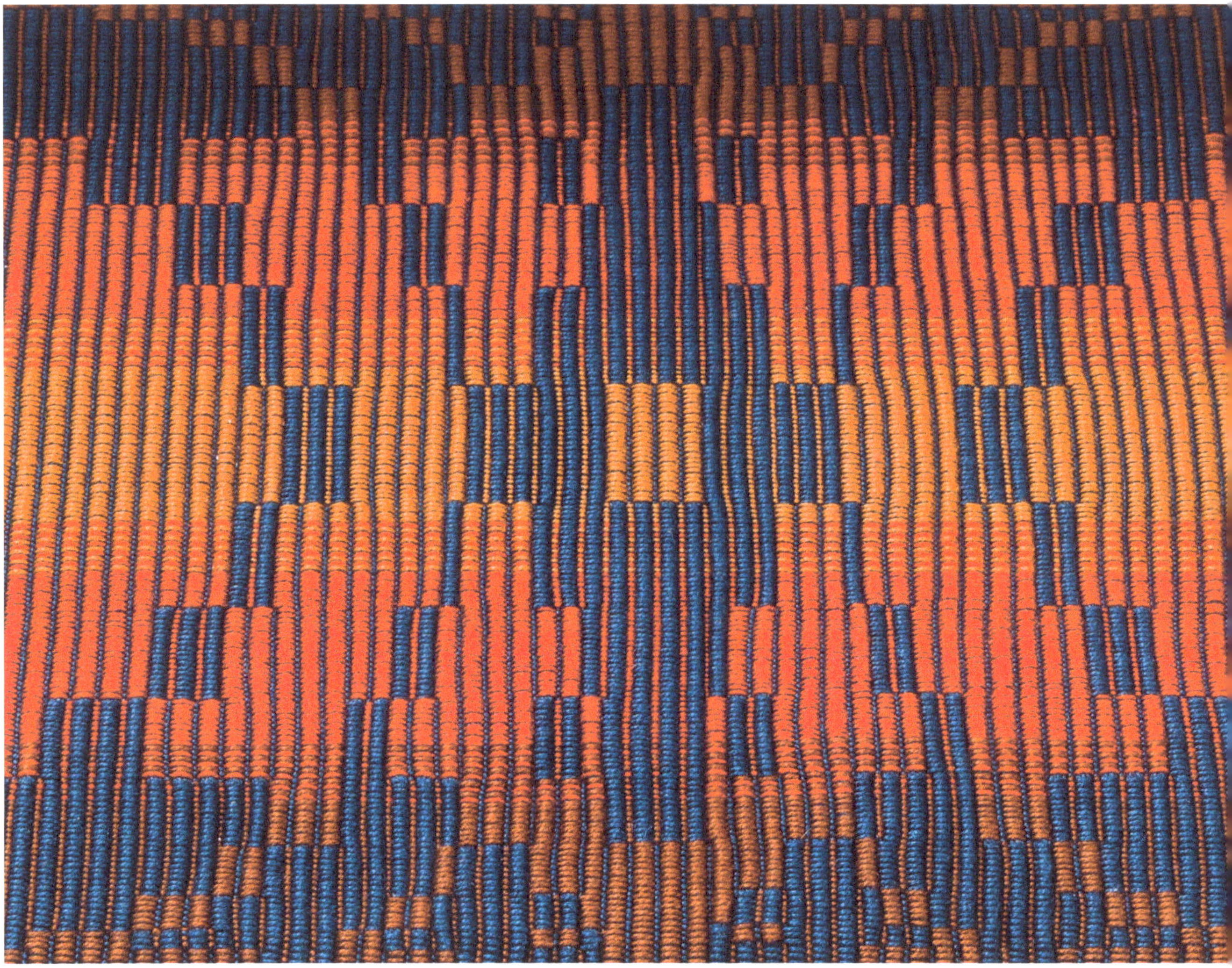

This cushion fits my bench perfectly, but you'll need to adjust the size for your own bench. Widen the side blocks or extend the treadling sequence to add extra length, as needed.

PROFILE DRAFT

C B A

H								H		
	G								G	
		F								
			E							
				D						
					C					
						B				
							A			
48	42	36	30	24	18	12	6	12	18	Ends per block

WARP COLOR SEQUENCE

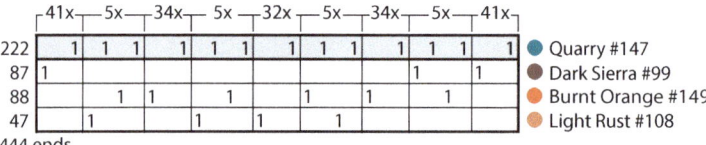

	41x	5x	34x	5x	32x	5x	34x	5x	41x	
222	1	1 1	1	1 1	1	1 1	1	1 1	1	Quarry #147
87	1							1	1	Dark Sierra #99
88		1	1	1		1	1	1		Burnt Orange #149
47		1		1	1	1				Light Rust #108

444 ends

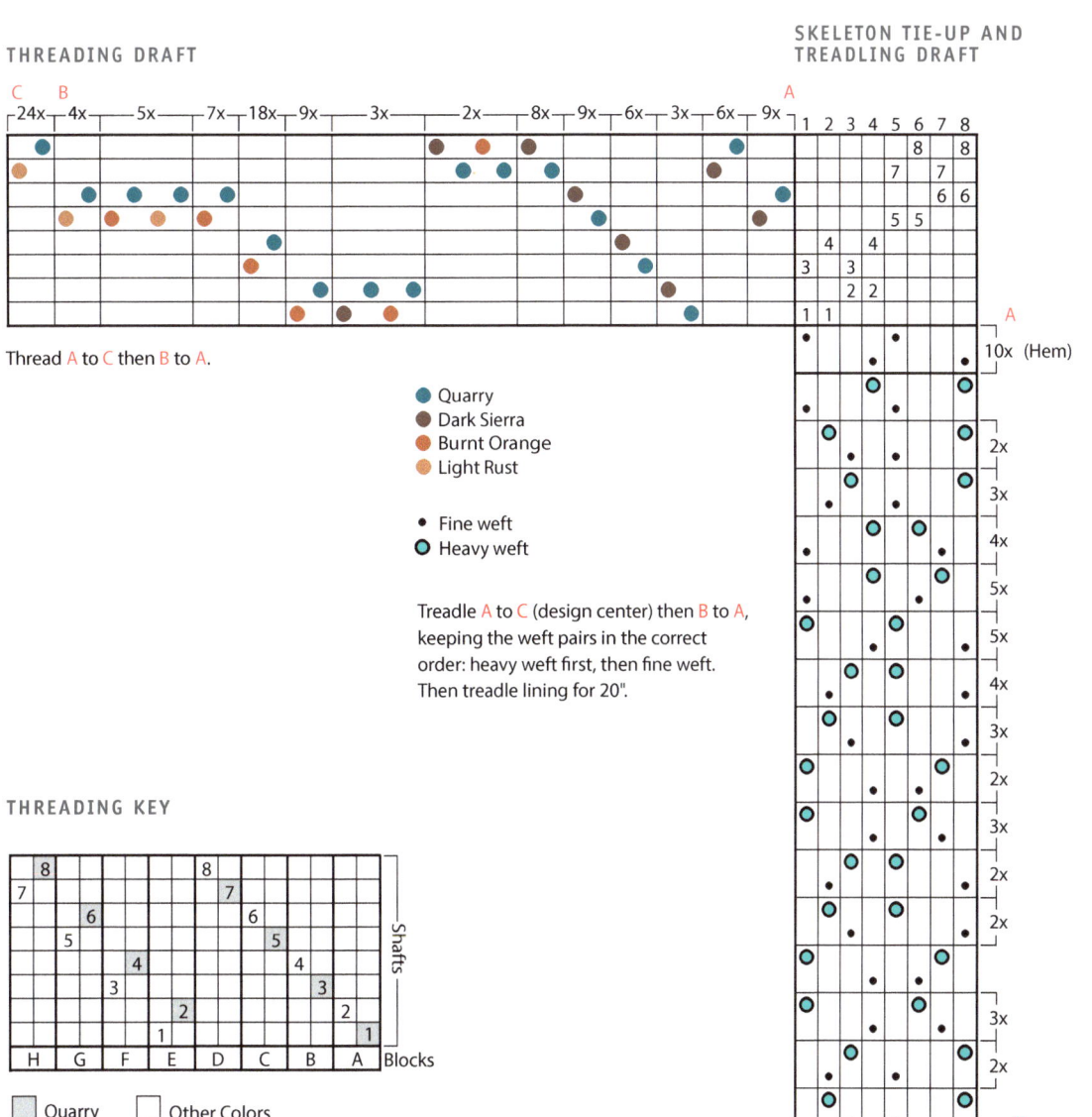

WEAVING

Start by weaving a small hem, then follow the treadling sequence. For the lining on the underside of the cushion, weave an additional 20 in. of plain weave with the fine weft, as shown in the draft.

FINISHING

Fill the lining with a thin foam pad and machine-stitch it to close. Attach the cushion to the bench with twisted or braided cords.

TABLE RUNNER AND MATS

Diamonds, Owl, Clown, and Butterfly

The set of weavings in this project comes from a long sampler that I offer to students in my workshop. These patterns are the most popular. The warp is a mix of gray and blue colors and long enough so you can sample variations on your own. "Diamonds" is shown on the facing page.

MATERIALS

Finished dimensions: Diamonds 10 in. x 15 in.; Owl 10 in. x 9 in.; Clown 10 in. x 11 in.; Butterfly 10 in. x 9 in.

Warp	5/2 mercerized cotton (UKI): Navy, Medium Grey, Birch, Poplin
Weft	
fine	10/2 mercerized cotton (UKI), Navy
heavy	11 threads of 5/2 mercerized cotton (UKI), Navy
Sett	40 epi
Reed	10 dents per inch
Sley	4 ends per dent; thread 1 end per heddle
Total ends	392
Width in reed	9.8 in.
Warp length	3 yd. *(loom waste included, with plenty extra to experiment)*
Weft sett	8 ribs (heavy and fine) per 2 in.
Length on loom	Diamonds 18 in.; Owl 12 in.; Clown 14 in.; Butterfly 12 in. *(under tension, hems included)*
Length off loom	Diamonds 17 in.; Owl 11 in.; Clown 13 in.; Butterfly 11 in.
Finished length	Diamonds 15 in.; Owl 9 in.; Clown 11 in.; Butterfly 9 in. *(washed, hemmed)*

PROFILE DRAFT

Thread A to C then B to A.

(Profile draft showing blocks A through H across 28 columns, 8 ends per block)

WARP COLOR SEQUENCE

	22x	6x	16x	6x	16x	6x	16x	6x	16x	6x	16x	6x	22x	
196	1	1	1	1	1	1	1	1	1	1	1	1	1	● Navy #15
56	1												1	● Medium Grey #19
56		1		1								1		Silver #141
56					1		1		1					Birch #74
28							1							Poplin #36

392 ends

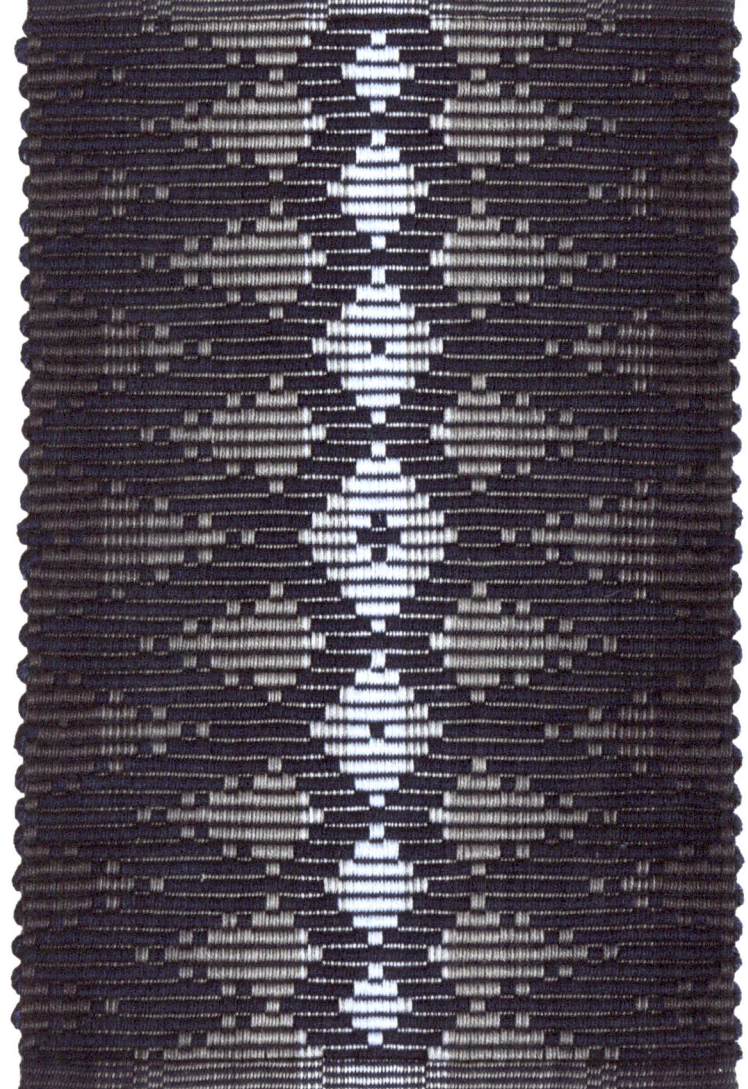

Diamonds

Treadling for Diamonds

(1) Begin with a hem.
(2) Treadle A to C, then B to A.
(3) Treadle C to E, then D to C.
(4) Treadle E to G, then F to E.
(5) Treadle G to I, then H to G.
(6) Reverse by repeating steps 4, 3, and 2.
(7) Finish with a hem.

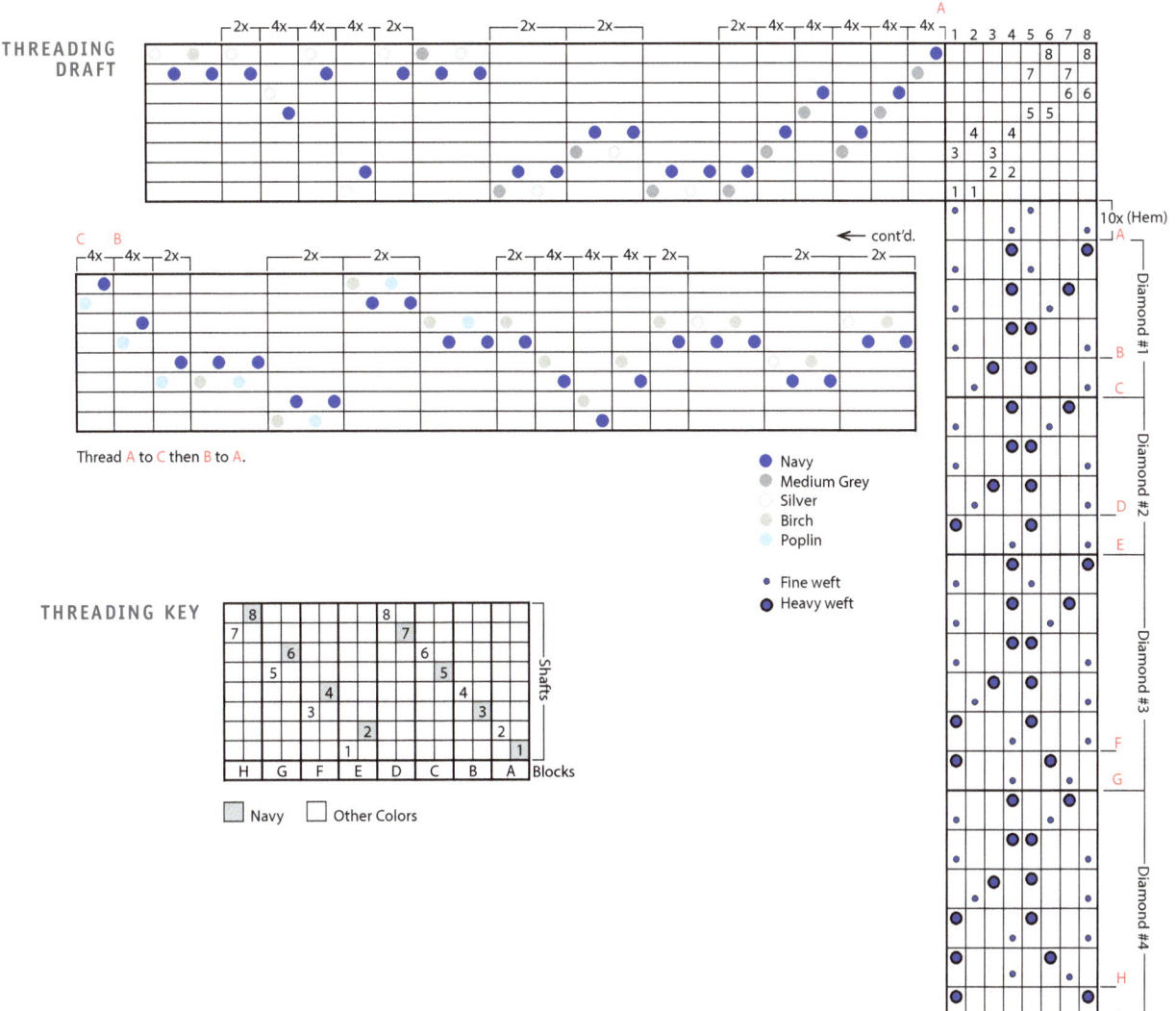

You might want to weave the Diamonds pattern to make placemats or extend the pattern to make a runner.

WEAVING

Start each piece with a small hem. Follow the treadling sequence carefully, keeping the weft pairs in the correct order as you reverse: heavy weft first, then fine weft. The small squares are not exactly symmetrical, so the treadling sequences are long.

Owl

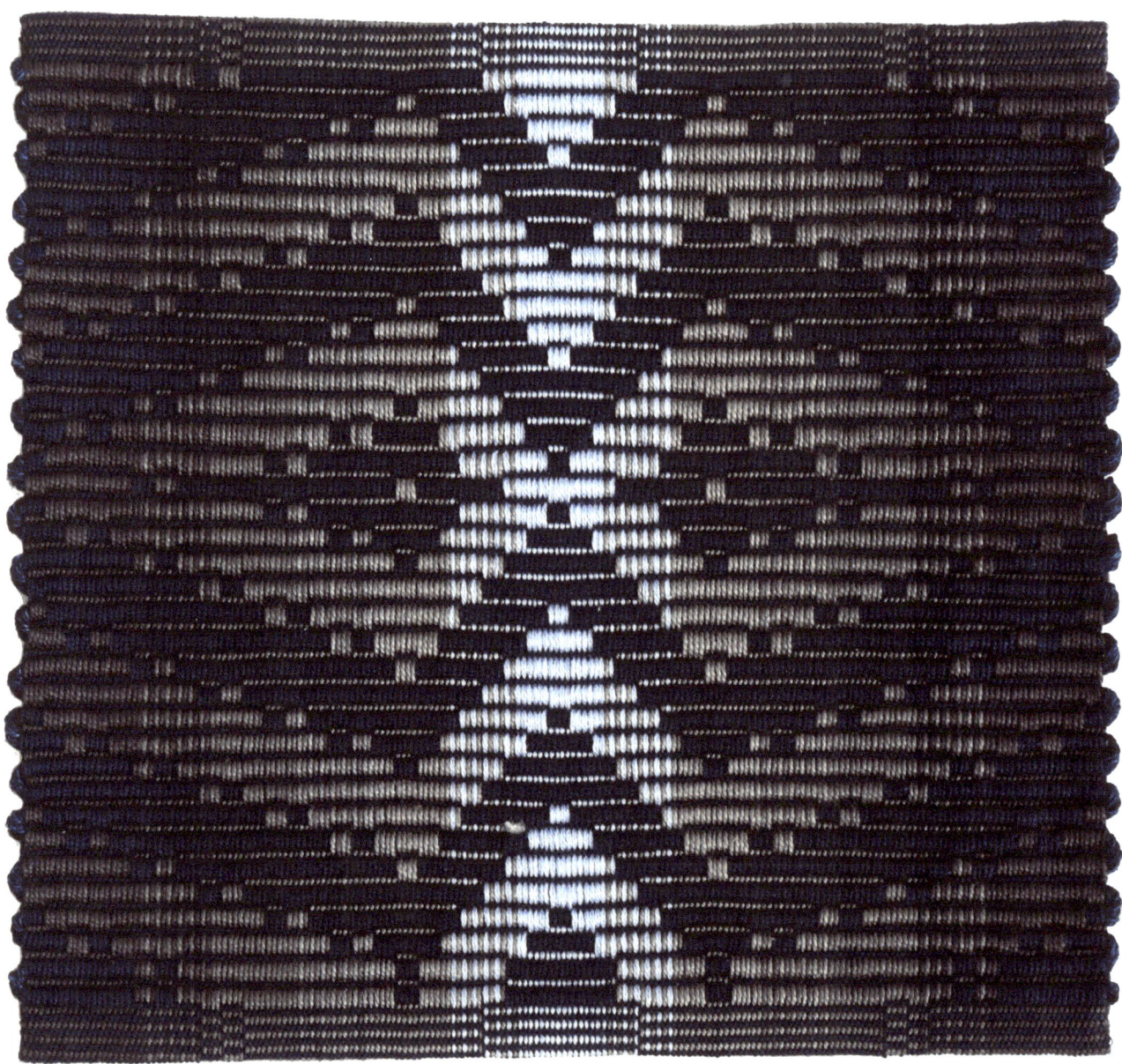

Treadling for Owl
(1) Begin with a hem.
(2) Treadle A to C.
(3) Treadle B to D.
(4) Treadle C to B, 2x.
(5) Finish with a hem.

Clown

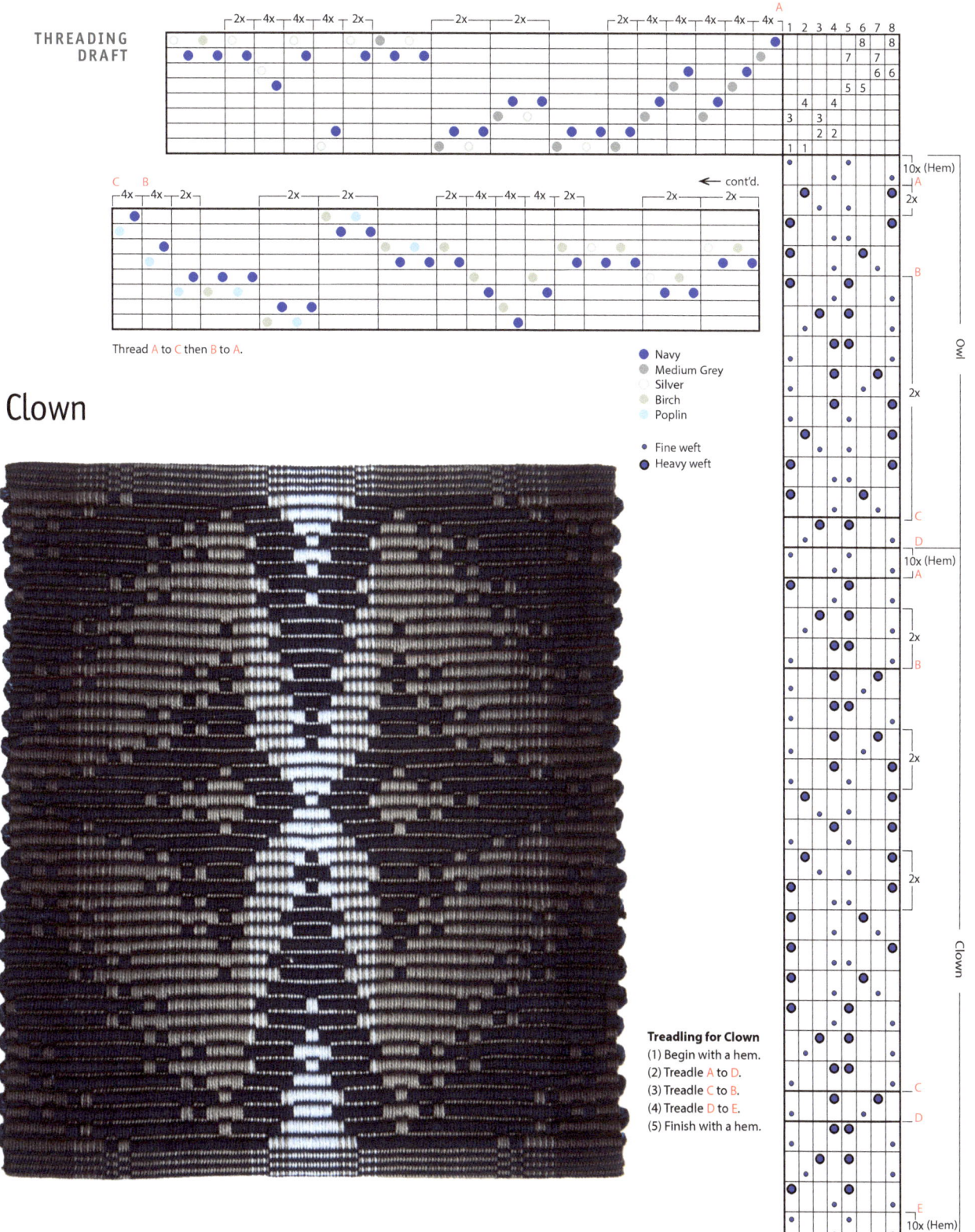

SKELETON TIE-UP AND TREADLING DRAFT

THREADING DRAFT

Thread A to C then B to A.

- Navy
- Medium Grey
- Silver
- Birch
- Poplin

· Fine weft
● Heavy weft

Treadling for Clown
(1) Begin with a hem.
(2) Treadle A to D.
(3) Treadle C to B.
(4) Treadle D to E.
(5) Finish with a hem.

EIGHT-SHAFT PROJECTS

Butterfly

SKELETON TIE-UP AND TREADLING DRAFT

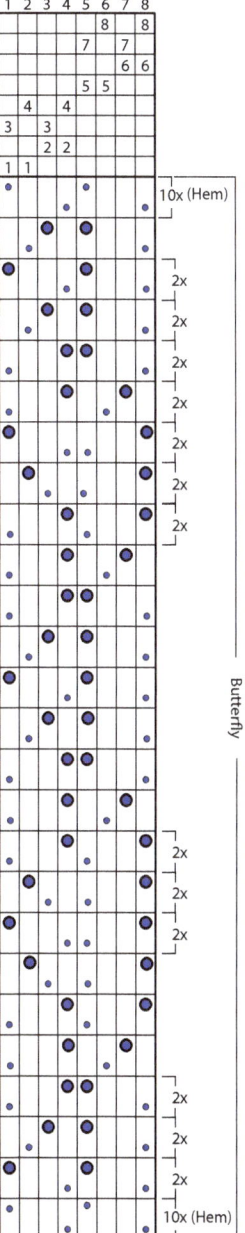

- • Fine weft
- ● Heavy weft

Treadling for Butterfly
Treadle as indicated in the draft, starting and finishing with a hem.

EIGHT-SHAFT PROJECTS

DESIGNING YOUR OWN PROJECTS

Planning a Rep Weave Pattern

PEOPLE FREQUENTLY ASK how and from where do I get my ideas for new projects. My main source for inspiration and design elements is nature. We are surrounded by patterns, motifs, and color combinations that we can use to form new designs.

Rep weave is a very linear weave, and many architectural designs can be a source of inspiration. A good starting point is to isolate a small motif within a larger one and repeating it in an overall design.

Old patterns in textiles can also be a source of inspiration—so traditional block weave patterns can easily be transcribed into rep weave (as for the design of "Undulations," page 103).

About Color

When you are looking through magazines, you may find landscape photographs that offer unusual shapes or blending of colors. It is important to experiment with different color arrangements. After many tries, you may feel comfortable with a color theme that you would never before have thought of trying.

It is always best to have strong contrast between the background color and the pattern. As I mention on page 11, in rep weaving think in terms of opposites: dark/light, background/pattern. In many of the projects in this book, I have used more than one color in the same block. Combining two shades adds depth and vibrancy—but if the warp is too complex, it's best to use only one color or a space-dyed color, which also creates a nice effect.

I like working with multiple colors so very often I choose a pattern warp that has many colors. When I am using several colors in the same spectrum, I alternate the threads for a width of ¼ in. in order to make a smooth transition between the different shades.

The Six Basic Design Steps

Here are six basic steps to follow as you plan your own rep weave design:

Step 1 Make a profile draft according to the order in which the blocks will be threaded and according to the width of each block.

Step 2 Decide on the yarn and the warp sett. Calculate the total number of warp threads for each project and the number of threads in each block. (To determine the right warp sett for your project, see page 13.)

Step 3 Establish the warp color sequence.

Step 4 Choose your threading key. Then create the threading draft according to the key.

Step 5 Establish the tie-up.

Step 6 Establish the treadling sequence for each block in your pattern to create the treadling draft. (To create new variations on a pattern, change the treadling and elongate the blocks.)

Designing a Two-Block Project

Here I am designing a set of four placemats in 8/4 carpet warp. The placemats are about 12 in. wide. The block pattern is A, B. The main color is navy with accents of blue, red, green, and yellow. The Dark Navy is a random mix of two shades from different dye lots. I chose a loose warp sett (24 epi) so as to keep the number of threads manageable. For a 12-in.-wide placemat, I needed a minimum of 288 ends:

24 epi x 12 in. = 288 ends

PLACEMAT LENGTH MEASUREMENTS

Length on loom: 22 in. *(under tension, hems included)*

Length off loom: 20.25 in.

Finished length: 18 in. *(washed, hemmed)*

Make the Profile Draft

Working with graph paper, I drew each block to the width I wanted for the design, labeling each as A or B. Each block spans a certain number of graph squares, or units. The sequence of A,B blocks in my pattern spans 73 units.

I divided the number of ends by the number of units to determine the number of ends in each square:

288 ends ÷ 73 units = 3.9 ends per unit

Because we are always working with pairs of threads, however, we cannot have a fractional or odd number of ends in a unit. I increased the number to **4 ends per unit**, so for this project I had a total of 292 ends. To maintain the width of the placemat, I had to make an adjustment. I decreased two of the A blocks by one unit, or 4 ends. The adjustment had very little visual impact on the finished design.

	B		B		B		B		B		B		
A		A		A		A		A		A		A	
36	8	36	8	32	8	36	8	32	8	36	8	36	292 ends
9	2	9	2	8	2	9	2	8	2	9	2	9	73 units

Determine the Warp Length

The finished length of each placemat is 18 in. I estimated roughly 26 in. of warp per placemat, including hems and tension take-up:

26 in. x 4 placemats = 104 inches = 2.88 yd.

The total length of the warp, factoring in loom waste of 24 in., would be 3.5 yd. To be on the safe side, I put a 4-yd.-long warp on the loom, which gave me plenty of extra warp for sampling, as needed. I dress the loom working from front to back, so I always begin by sleying the reed.

For this design, I used a 12-dent reed. With a sett of 24 epi, I sleyed 2 ends per dent.

Create the Warp Color Sequence (color key)

It is easier and faster to make the warp by using 1 thread of the top layer and 1 thread of the bottom layer. Sley the pair together in each dent. They will be separated when you thread the heddles.

Make the warp from A to C and then reverse B to A. When reversing, always keep this sequence: top layer thread first, then bottom layer thread.

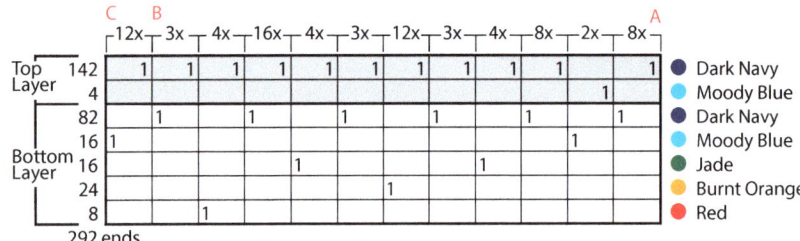

Choose the Threading Key

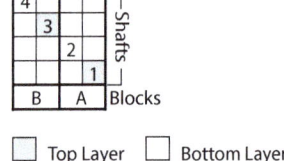

There are several possibilities for threading on four shafts. I chose the sequence at left, which is one of my favorites. The squares are shaded or unshaded to indicate the layer.

Determine the Threading Draft

Follow the threading key to create the threading draft. The threading draft shows the weave pattern from its beginning (A) to its center (C). To complete the pattern, reverse threading from B to A, continuing to alternate odd/even shafts (top/bottom layers). When you reverse from B to A, you will begin again with the top layer.

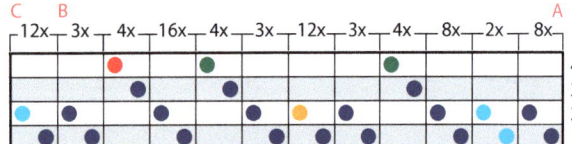

Establish the Tie-Up

There are four treadling possibilities for this threading key. I chose the tie-up shown here. Each block has its own tie-up. Treadle 1 creates the solid navy line across the placemat pattern. Treadle 2 will bring up Block B. Treadle 3 will bring up Block A. Treadle 4 will bring up both blocks.

Treadles	1	2	3	4
		4		4
	3		3	
			2	2
	1	1		
Blocks		B	A	A+B

Create the Treadling Draft

As you can see from the treadling draft at right, this placemat (like every project in this book) starts with a hem made with the fine weft only, using treadles 1 and 4.

The solid warp lines can be threaded as any block, but I chose to thread them as Block A. When the block changes in the treadling, a fine weft thread will be in the same shed as the new heavy weft thread.

I have provided only one treadling sequence for this sample placemat. I hope you will experiment to find variations.

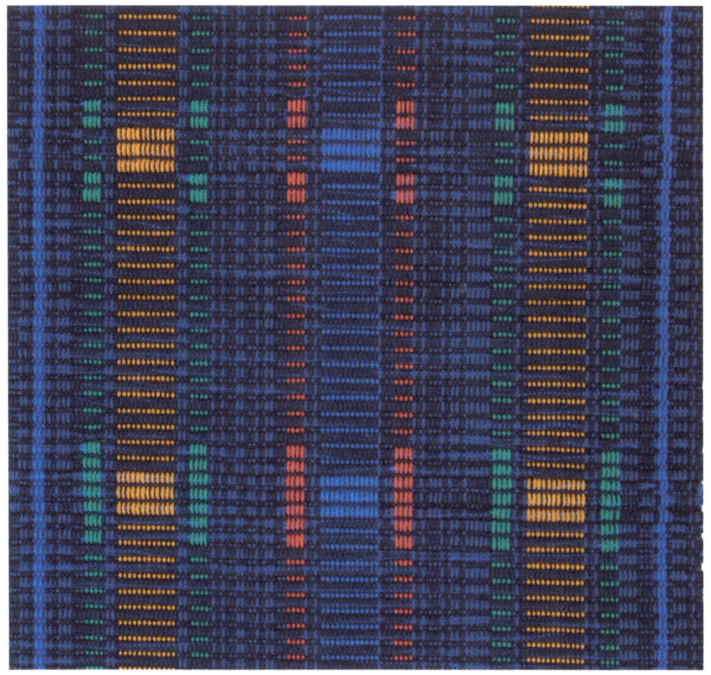

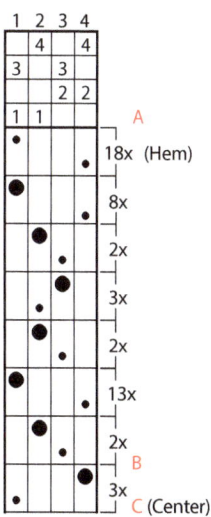

- Fine weft
- Heavy weft

Treadle A to C, then B to A, always keeping the weft pairs in the correct order: heavy weft first, then fine weft.

DESIGNING YOUR OWN PROJECTS

Designing a Four-Block Project

These potholders are good projects for trying out new patterns. They are relatively easy to plan: the number of threads is low and the weaving is fast. Besides they make great little gifts.

Each of these potholders measures approximately 8.5 in. x 8.5 in. There's enough warp for eight potholders (four pairs). They are made with 5/2 mercerized cotton with a sett of 40 epi. I needed approximately 340 ends.

8.5 in. x 40 epi = 340 ends

POTHOLDER MEASUREMENTS

These measurements are the same for each potholder:

Length on loom: 11 in. *(under tension, hems included)*

Length off loom: 10 in.

Finished length: 8.5 in. *(washed, hemmed)*

Make the Profile Draft

Working with graph paper, I drew each block to the width I wanted for the design, labeling each. The four-block pattern spans 28 units.

340 ends ÷ 28 units = 12.1 ends per unit

To avoid the fraction, I rounded down to **12 threads per unit**. Each square on the profile draft represents 12 threads: 6 from the top layer, 6 from the bottom layer. Working with a 10-dent reed, I sleyed 2 pairs of threads per dent but a single thread in the heddle.

Border						Center				Border					
D		D	D		D				D		D	D		D	
	C			C			B			C			C		
						A		A							
24	24	12	12	12	24	24	24	24	24	24	12	12	12	24	24	336 ends
2	2	1	1	1	2	2	2	2	2	2	1	1	1	2	2	28 units

Determine the Warp Length

I needed 11 in. of warp per potholder.

11 in. × 8 potholders = 88 in.

After adding 24 in. of loom waste, I rounded up to the next quarter-yard and used a total warp length of 3.25 yd.

Create the Warp Color Sequence (color key)

When creating the warp color sequence, I always choose one color that I will include in every block (here the color is UKI Medium Brown #25). I assign contrasting colors to the same blocks in each pattern repeat. In this draft, the A, B, A blocks form the central pattern.

	12x	12x	6x	6x	6x	12x	12x	12x	12x	12x	12x	6x	6x	6x	12x	12x	
168	1		1		1		1		1		1		1		1	1	● Medium Brown #25
60	1					1			1							1	● Light Rust #108
84		1		1			1			1		1		1			● Old Gold #29
24				1				1			1		1				● Lipstick #32
	D	C	D	C	D	C	D	A	B	A	D	C	D	C	D	D	Blocks

336 ends

Choose the Threading Key

When creating four blocks on four shafts, two blocks use the same pair of shafts but in the reverse order:

Block A: Shaft #1 for Background Color   Shaft #2 for Pattern Color
Block B: Shaft #3 for Background Color   Shaft #4 for Pattern Color
Block C: Shaft #2 for Background Color   Shaft #1 for Pattern Color
Block D: Shaft #4 for Background Color   Shaft #3 for Pattern Color

Determine the Threading Draft

The threading key establishes the threading draft. The draft is a thread-by-thread guide, providing the order in which the threads are brought through the heddles. The numbers along the top indicate the width of the block, as determined by the profile draft.

Note that the Medium Brown end is always threaded first, followed by a contrasting warp thread. This threading draft shows the entire potholder pattern.

- Medium Brown #25
- Light Rust #108
- Old Gold #29
- Lipstick #32

Establish the Tie-Up

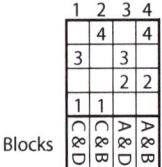

There are four treadling possibilities for these potholders. Each one will affect two blocks at the same time. Note that when using treadle 1, Blocks C and D are affected. When using the opposite treadle—treadle 4—Blocks A and B are affected.

Create the Treadling Draft

Here is the treadling sequence for one potholder. By varying the treadling sequence and the number of repetitions, you can achieve a variety of designs.

I usually count how many ribs I will need to square the potholders. For these I needed 27 to 28 ribs. You will need to experiment to get the right size. Don't forget that you need to elongate the piece in order to be sure to have the correct size when the weaving is off the loom and no longer under tension.

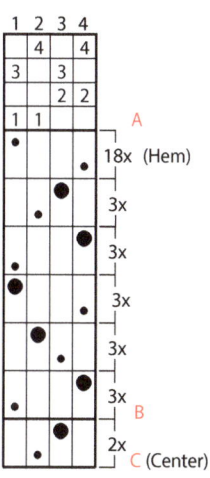

- Fine weft
- Heavy weft

Treadle A to C, then B to A, always keeping the weft pairs in the correct order: heavy weft first, then fine weft.

Game Boards and Mazes

REP WEAVE IS A VERY LINEAR WEAVE and lends itself to many grid-like projects. In this chapter I am presenting some fun projects to weave as a source of inspiration for your own projects. I strongly recommend and challenge you to give them a try.

Game Boards

We have seen more than one checkerboard woven in rep weave or other weaving techniques. My first attempt was published in *Handwoven* magazine in 2005 ("Checkers, Anyone? A Rep Runner for Holiday Games"). Since then I have made quite a few and I really enjoy refining and adding to the design.

My most recent version was a set of four game boards that we sometimes use when we are in our cabin in Vermont. All the boards were made on the same warp—5/2 mercerized cotton, sett at 40 epi—and were rethreaded as needed for the individual pattern. The finished sizes are 16 in. x 16 in., requiring 640 ends. The weft of each is 12 ends of 5/2 black mercerized cotton.

This **Traditional Checkerboard** requires only four shafts. You will need to sample the heavy weft in order to get the perfect balance of thickness to square the playing tiles. After I made this game board, I had some leftover warp, so I made another checkerboard mat and the perfect little checkers pouch to store the playing pieces.

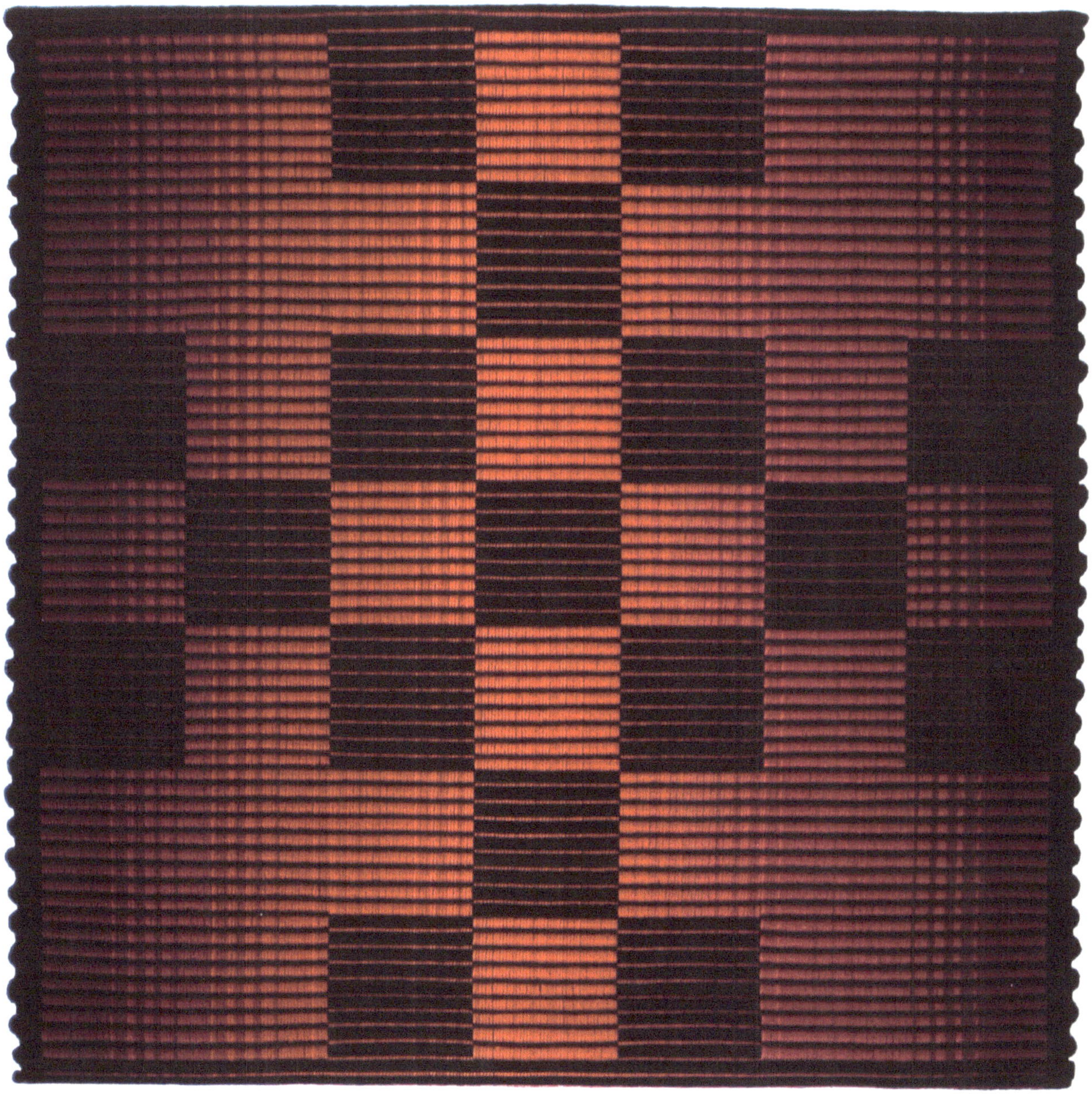

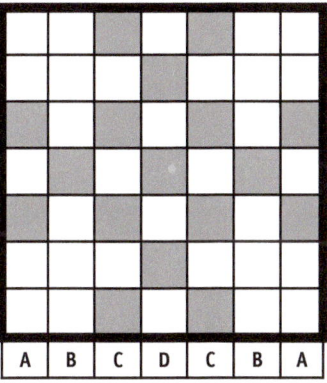

This **Solitaire Board** needs eight shafts, a recalculation of the block width, and, of course, rethreading. Because all the boards are the same size, these squares are a little wider.

LET'S PLAY

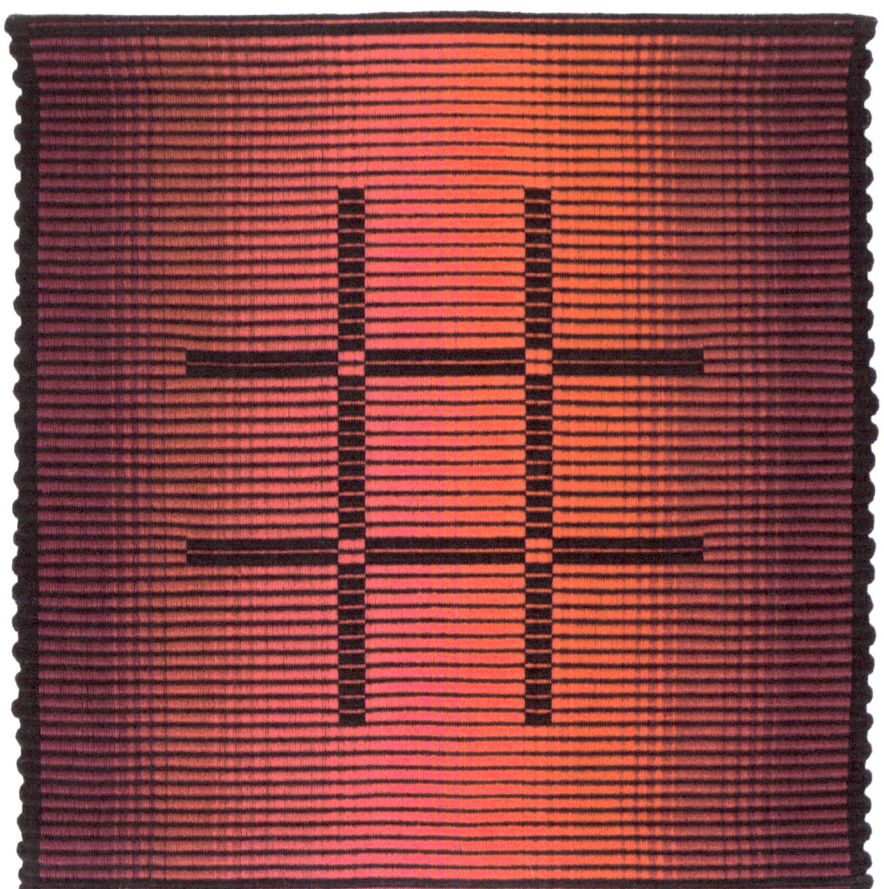

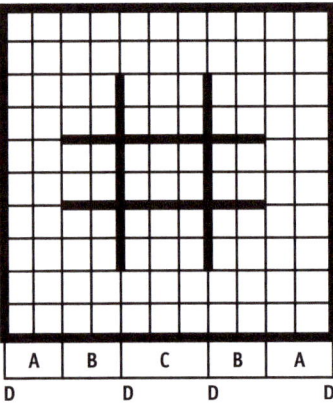

This **Tic-Tac-Toe Game Board** is another easy and fun board to weave. It requires only four shafts, but if you are using an eight-shaft loom, it's a good idea to spread the blocks over more than two shafts.

PICKING UP

This method of picking up is very similar to the one used in double weave. In this description, the red threads are pattern threads and the black threads are the background threads.

When weaving the heavy weft, raise all red threads and pick up the design, always working with pairs of threads. Leave the pick-up stick in place.

Raise all black threads Place a sword into the shed, making sure to insert it also under the selected red threads.

Place the sword on its side to create a shed. Weave the heavy weft shot.

When weaving the fine weft, raise all black threads and pick up the design, always working with corresponding pairs of threads. Leave the pick-up stick in place.

Raise all red threads. Place a sword into the shed and manipulate it under the black picked-up threads. Place the sword on its side to create the shed. Weave the fine weft shot.

The game of Windmill may not be as well known in the United States but it is very popular in Europe. This **Windmill Game Board** requires eight shafts and a lot of pick-ups. If you have access to a sixteen-shaft loom, the weaving will be easier, but you will still need the help of picking up.

LET'S PLAY

Hop, Skip, and Jump Rug

My most recent project was inspired by having to make a rug for the bunk-bed room in our Vermont cabin. Given the dimensions of the room, the rug had to be a long narrow runner. I also wanted it to be fun design for my grandchildren who would be sleeping there.

My initial idea was to weave a hopscotch design, but the numbers were too difficult to pick up in rep weave. After a bit of brainstorming, I finally realized that I could use dots instead of numbers—just as on dice.

I used carpet warp in two colors, navy and blue/gray, at a sett of 30 epi. To start I made a diagram of the squares and the dots. The finished piece evolved from there and varies slightly from the diagram.

I decided to use four shafts for the wider spaces to help with the weaving because the warp was very sticky. I picked up all the dots, but the hardest part was centering them in the big squares through trial and error.

The finished rug is 33 in. wide and 98 in. long. After the rug was woven, I decided to make little tiles containing the initials of my grandchildren's names. I wove the tiles in red and gray on my small loom and filled them with pebbles to give them weight.

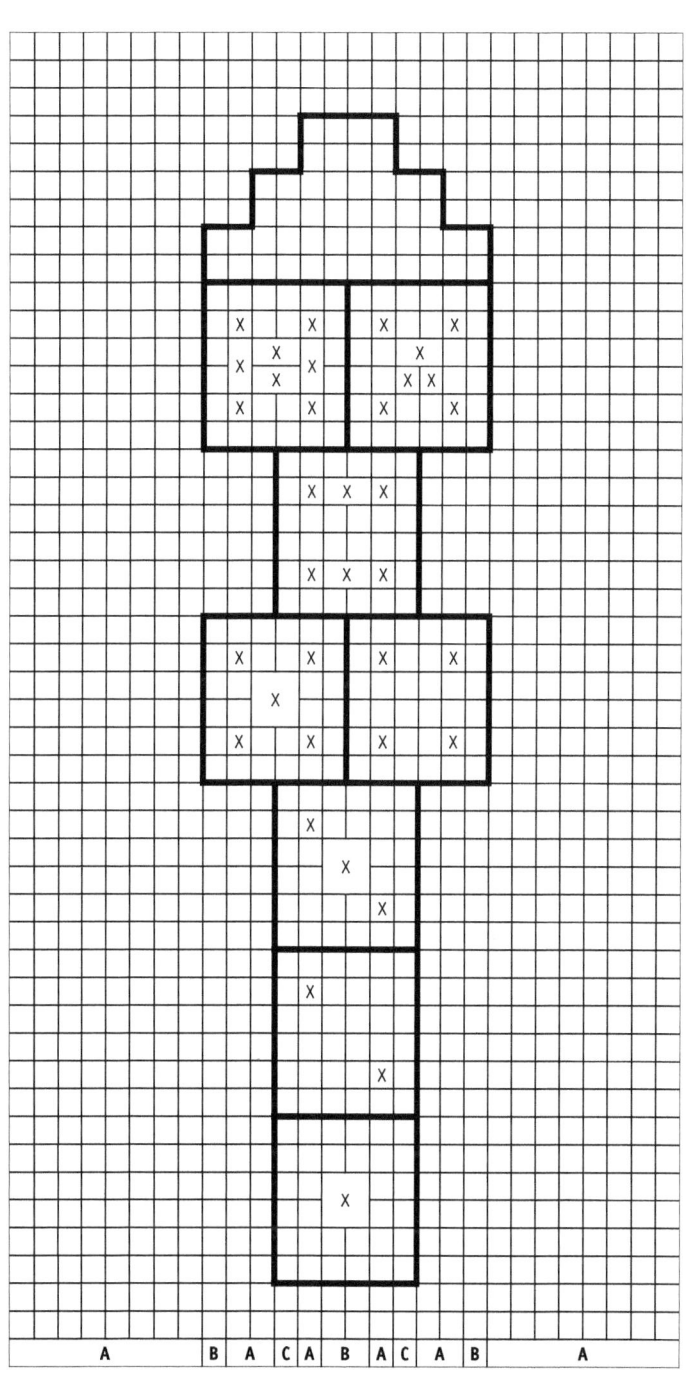

LET'S PLAY 151

Tapu'at Maze

Since childhood, I have always been fascinated by mazes—another design I thought would be perfect for rep weave. Several years ago I was asked to make a wall hanging for the Physicians Building at Yale University. I was told the piece would hang in the waiting room of the Department of Fertility and Reproductive Sciences.

I thought that a maze would be perfect wall hanging for patients to look at during their wait, allowing them to stare into space or possibly to challenge themselves to attempt to follow the path.

In the book *The Art of the Maze* by Adrian Fisher and Georg Gerster, I found a labyrinth that the Hopi Tribe uses called *Tapu'at* ("Mother and Child"), a design symbolizing the mother enclosing her child. I felt it would be a perfect fit for the place where this piece would be displayed.

I made this wall hanging in many colors of 5/2 mercerized cotton, with a sett of 48 epi. I wove it on my 60-in., eight-shaft Leclerc Colonial loom, using many pick-ups (see page 148). To achieve the square shape of this piece, I had to make many careful calculations. I was constantly checking and counting. I greatly enjoyed making this piece because it was both challenging and inspiring.

Labyrinth of Color

After weaving the "*Tapu'at* Maze," I had a lot of warp left on the loom. I saved the warp in three chains and eventually decided to make a triptych. I used one chain of warp for each panel.

First I designed a maze for one panel and wove it. Then I designed and wove the second and third panels. Each panel is connected to the next, to form a stepped pattern. Because of the gradations of color, I named this maze "Labyrinth of Color."

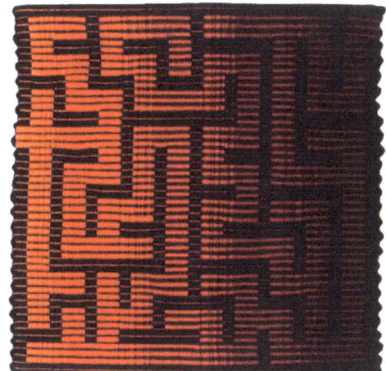

THREE-DIMENSIONAL FORMS

Books, Bags, and Boxes

AS YOU HAVE LEARNED from the projects featured in this book, rep weave is a very linear weave. The ribs that characterize the weave structure also lend themselves easily to bending and folding.

In this section I'll share some of the three-dimensional rep weave projects that I have devised. I hope they will be a source of inspiration as you begin to design your own projects.

Book or iPad Cover

Several years ago I received a very nice drafting pad from one of my students. I didn't care much for the cover, but the printed sheets were nicely designed for weaving projects. As I had some leftover warp on the loom that was just the right width, I wove a piece of rep fabric for the cover and an additional length of fine plain weave for the lining.

I hand-sewed the cover and lining and reinforced the inside pocket with some stiff cardboard. I finished the piece with a nice clasp.

I continue to make book and iPad covers from the materials I have left over from other projects.

THREE-DIMENSIONAL FORMS

Two Bags

The stiffness of rep weave is perfect for making bags of all sorts. I have made many styles, but here are a few specialty bags that I frequently use.

Although I had never used Tencel for rep weaving, it seems to be the perfect material for a lightweight **Jewelry Pouch** (shown this page). By alternating bands of rep weave and plain weave, I constructed several pockets for necklaces and bracelets.

I always travel with a few knitting accessories, but more often than not I leave home with the wrong-size needles and need to purchase a new set. With the warp left over from some placemats I made, I wove some rep weave fabric for the outside of this **Knitting Needles Bag** (shown on facing page). I switched to plain weave to make the lining. I hand-sewed the two pieces together and made pockets for the needles. Then I just finished it with some braids to tie the bag together. The roll is not too bulky to take along in a weekend bag.

Three Little Boxes

The structure and texture of rep weave lends itself to making rigid squares. I thought that I could build a box, using two rectangles that intersect each other. It was critical to take careful measurements. The diagram illustrates how the box was constructed. By alternating rep-weave parts with plain-weave parts, I wove two long rectangles.

I needed something rigid to hold the sides and found that balsa wood was the perfect material. It is firm, lightweight, and easy to cut to shape. I used the wood for the sides and the base, between the bottom two layers.

These three boxes serve different purposes. The name of the first one, **Odds and Ends** (shown this page), says it all. **Secretary** (facing page) holds a pen and writing paper. **Jewelry Box** (page 162) has a soft padded interior for storing fine jewelry.

This diagram gives measurements for the finished size for Secretary. Vary the sizes to make the other boxes. Note that the bottom inside piece of the base is smaller than the outside piece. The plain-weave lining can be adjusted to make a perfect fit.

SIDES AND BOTTOM LINING

160 REP RIPS REPS WEAVE

162 REP RIPS REPS WEAVE

Appendix: More Drafting Styles

I have used one kind of draft throughout this book. You may see other styles in other weaving books, so I wanted to mention them here. Experiment with the different methods yourself and find the one that is best suited to your own style of weaving.

Threading and Tie-Up Styles

There are three ways to write the threading drafts for a basic two-block rep weave on four shafts. Keep in mind that the shaded boxes (X) represent the top layer, or background. The unshaded boxes (O) represent the bottom layer, or pattern. Each of the methods has a different tie-up.

I. The Style I Prefer

This is the style you'll find most often in this book. I prefer to use this threading style because it's easier to thread a block on adjacent shafts—in other words, shafts 1 and 2 work as a pair to weave Block A; shafts 3 and 4 work as a pair to weave Block B. I start all projects with a fine hem, which is woven using treadles 1 and 4 (the threads are not adjacent and therefore the shafts are easier to lift).

				Shafts
O				4
	X			3
		O		2
			X	1
B		A		Blocks

X = Top Layer   O = Bottom Layer

Treadles	1	2	3	4
		4		4
	3		3	
			2	2
	1	1		
Blocks		B	A	A+B

II. Styles for Wide Blocks

This threading draft style is the one you'll often find in books and magazines. "Rail Tracks," page 52, "Theme Variations," page 79, and "Adding Colors," page 83, are threaded this way. This method is useful when there are many threads in the same block because it avoids threading through adjacent shafts.

				Shafts
0				4
		0		3
	X			2
			X	1
	B		A	Blocks

X = Top Layer   0 = Bottom Layer

Treadles	1	2	3	4
		4		4
		3	3	
	2		2	
	1			1
Blocks		A+B	A	B

III. The Scandinavian Method

This threading draft style is the one found most often in Swedish rep weaving books. Some weavers may find it a little confusing to thread pairs of shafts that are so far apart.

				Shafts
		0		4
0				3
	X			2
			X	1
	B		A	Blocks

X = Top Layer   0 = Bottom layer

Treadles	1	2	3	4
		4	4	
		3		3
	2		2	
	1			1
Blocks		A+B	A	B

Drafting Four Blocks on Four Shafts

You can design a four-block rep weave pattern on four shafts, but in order to do so, two blocks will use the same pair of shafts (although in reverse order). The position of the color warp threads differentiates the blocks.

I. The American Way

In the most common drafting method, which I call the American Way, Block A uses shaft 1 for the dark color. In Block C, shaft 1 holds the light or contrasting color. In Block B, shaft 3 holds the dark color, and in Block D shaft 3 holds the light or contrasting color. With this method, you cannot weave a block by itself and cannot have a solid dark area across the width of the fabric.

Notice that the dark and light threads always follow each other when running from one block to the other.

						Shafts
	X		O			4
O				X		3
		X			O	2
		O			X	1
D	C	B	A	Blocks

THE AMERICAN WAY TIE-UP

1	2	3	4	Treadles
		4	4	
3	3			
	2		2	
1		1		
C+D	A+D	B+C	A+B	Blocks

II. The Scandinavian Method

Unlike the American Way, the Scandinavian Method positions two light threads next to each other, between Blocks B and C, as marked. The doubling of dark threads occurs between Blocks D and A. This doubling of light threads and dark threads will cause a slight line in the weaving, which detracts from the overall design.

					Shafts
X				O	4
	X		O		3
		O	X		2
	O			X	1
D	C	B	A		Blocks

SCANDINAVIAN METHOD TIE-UP

1	2	3	4	Treadles
	4	4		
	3		3	
2		2		
1			1	
C+D	A+B	A+C	B+D	Blocks

Drafting Four Blocks on Eight Shafts

The Traditional Threading Method is the one I used for all of the four-block, eight-shaft projects in this book.

This method uses the same rules as for two blocks on four shafts. Each block uses two adjacent shafts. I prefer this method because it is easier to weave the hems by lifting every other shaft.

TRADITIONAL THREADING METHOD

					Shafts
8					8
	7				7
		6			6
			5		5
			4		4
				3	3
				2	2
				1	1
D	C	B	A		Blocks

The traditional tie-up is most often used when blocks are woven individually. When blocks are combined, you may need to go under the loom to re-tie the treadles.

TRADITIONAL TIE-UP

1	2	3	4	5	6	7	8	9	10	Treadles
	8		8		8		8	8		
7		7		7		7			7	
	6		6		6	6			6	
5		5		5			5	5		
	4	4			4		4		4	
3			3	3		3		3		
2			2		2		2		2	
	1	1		1		1		1		
A	B			Plain Weave		C		D		Blocks

With four blocks on eight shafts, there are sixteen different combinations possible and ten treadles. It is best to use a skeleton tie-up, because the treadling is done with both feet. When depressing the treadles one after the other, you will get a cleaner shed—and the weaving is easier on the loom, too.

THE SKELETON TIE-UP

1	2	3	4	5	6	7	8	Treadle #
					8		8	
				7		7		
						6	6	
				5	5			
	4		4					
3		3						
		2	2					
1	1							
Left foot				Right foot				

Here is an alternate way to thread four blocks on eight shafts. I rarely use this threading key because I find the treadling much more difficult. If you wanted to weave a hem, you would have to lift four adjacent shafts (1, 2, 3, 4), which would put a lot of stress on the warp.

ALTERNATE THREADING METHOD

					Shafts
8					8
	7				7
		6			6
			5		5
4					4
	3				3
		2			2
			1		1
D	C	B	A		Blocks

Yarn Sources

Great Northern Weaving
(8/4 carpet warp, 4/4 cotton, heavy weft)
451 East D Avenue
Kalamazoo, MI 49009
www.greatnorthernweaving.com
800.446.5977

Halcyon Yarn
(3/2 pearl cotton, 5/2 pearl cotton, 8/4 carpet warp)
12 School Street
Bath, ME 04530
www.halcyonyarn.com
800.341.0282

Lunatic Fringe Yarns
(10/2 pearl cotton, 2/8 cotton, heavy weft)
2291 SW 2nd Avenue
Fruitland, ID 83619
www.lunaticfringeyarns.com
800.483.8749

UKI Supreme Corporation
(5/2 pearl cotton, 10/2 pearl cotton)
325 Spencer Road
Conover, NC 28613
www.ukisupreme.com
888.604.6975

Vävstuga LLC
(string yarn, mini, midi, maxi, heavy weft)
16 Water Street
Shelburne Falls, MA 01370
www.vavstuga.com
413.625.8241

WEBS
(3/2 pearl cotton, 5/2 pearl cotton, 8/2 Tencel)
75 Service Center Road
Northampton, MA 01060
www.yarn.com
800.367.9327

Yarn Barn
(3/2 pearl cotton, 5/2 pearl cotton, 8/4 carpet warp)
930 Massachusetts Street
Lawrence, KS 66044
www.yarnbarn-ks.com
800.468.0035

Recommended Books

Carlstedt, Catharina, and Ylva Kongback. *REP*. Helsingborg, Sweden: AB Boktryck, 1987.
Lundell, Laila. *Rep Weaves*. Vasteras, Sweden: ICA-förlaget AB, 1987.
Marshall, Kelly. *Custom Woven Interiors*. Minneapolis, MN: Custom Woven Interiors Ltd, 2012.
Proulx, Bibiane April. *Reps*. Quebec, Canada: Les Editions La Tirelle, 1979.
Tallarovic, Joanne. *Rep Weave and Beyond*. Loveland, CO: Interweave Press, 2004.

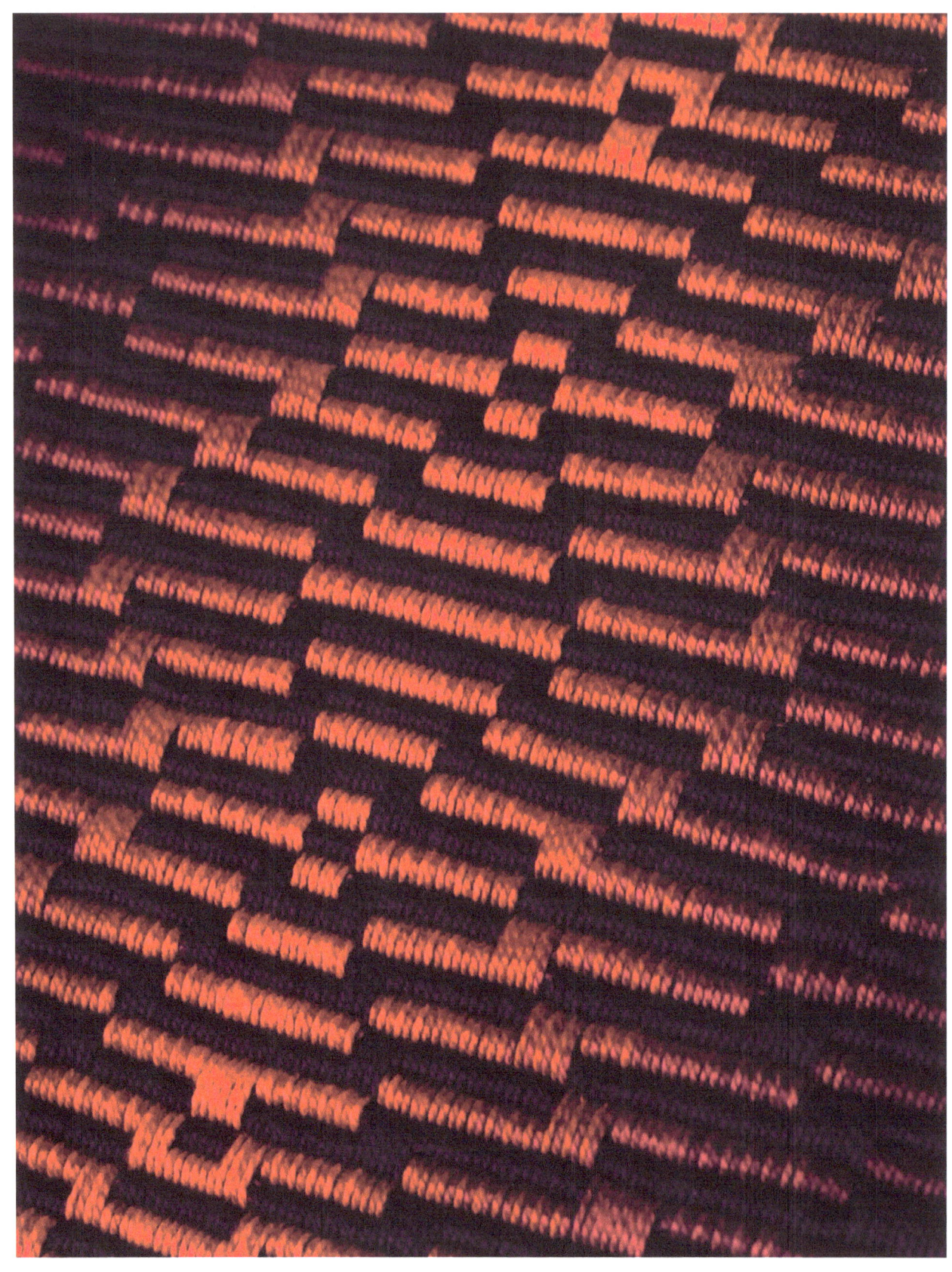

About the Author

Lucienne Coifman, a former research assistant in biochemistry, is self-taught in the art of weaving. She has been developing and teaching her rep weave methods and designs for more than thirty years. Her work has appeared in *Handwoven* and *Shuttle Spindle and Dyepot* magazines and in juried exhibitions in Europe and throughout the United States.

For a listing of her workshops and a photo gallery of her work, visit her website: lucienne-repweave.com.

Lucienne invites readers to send their questions and comments about *Rep, Rips, Reps: Projects, Instruction, and Inspiration* to her at info@lucienne-repweave.com.

Index

A
Alternate Threading Method: 168
American Way drafting method: 165
arching: 21, 33, 37, 45
Art of the Maze, The: 152

B
background *(top)* layer: 11, 19, 24, 25, 29, 41, 73, 75, 88, 110, 113, 134, 138, 141, 142, 148, 163
beat:
  hard: 29, 47, 109, 111
  maintaining steady: 22, 37, 55
beater: 11, 29
bengaline weave structure: 29, 42, 45
binding *(or tie-down)* weft: 9, 11, 15, 23
block width: 24, 25, 73, 79, 135, 137, 141, 142, 147, 164
blocks:
  elongating: 15, 19, 22, 37, 89, 135, 143
  large: 47, 52, 55, 69, 164
  squaring: 15, 22, 62, 89, 143, 146
  transition between: 21, 33, 41, 59, 63, 73, 77, 139, 166
books: 152, 169
bottom layer: See *pattern (bottom) layer.*
braiding: 23, 123, 158

C
chair covers: 91, 92–95
checkerboard: 19, 146
color, solid line of: 24, 25, 47, 57, 58, 61, 63, 97, 139, 165
color key: See *warp color sequence (color key).*
colors:
  blending: 15, 87, 134
  choosing: 10, 12, 13, 14, 19, 66, 67, 69, 87, 97, 134, 136, 141
  mixing: 15, 47, 61, 65, 69, 89, 97, 103, 109, 110, 125, 134, 136

D
design inspiration: 133, 151, 152
design steps: 135
double-thread method: 12, 13, 73, 87, 88, 89, 91, 109, 110

E
ends per inch (epi): 13, 29, 136, 137, 140
épinglé weave structure: 29, 42, 45

F
finishing: 23, 77, 123, 158
fringe: 23, 52, 75, 77

G
games: 145, 146–149, 151

H
Handwoven magazine: 91, 146
heddles: 11, 20, 25, 40, 44, 73, 88, 110, 138, 141, 142
hems: 19, 22, 23, 52, 54, 77, 94, 106, 118, 139, 163, 167

J
Jewelry Box: 160, 162
Jewelry Pouch: 158

K
Knitting Needles Bag: 158, 159

L
labyrinths: 152, 153
layers: See *background (top) layer* and *pattern (bottom) layer.*
length:
  extending: 22, 122, 127
  measuring: 19, 22, 37, 49, 50, 55, 80, 94, 118
lining: 113, 121, 123, 157, 158, 160
loom:
  bench cushion for: 121–123
  dressing from front to back: 20, 44, 88, 110, 137
  selection: 11, 29, 148, 151, 152
  setup: 17, 20–21
loom waste: 19, 137, 141

M
materials: 11, 12–13, 15
mazes: 152, 153
metallic thread: 57, 61
Mother and Child *(Tapu'at)* maze: 152, 153

O
Odds and Ends box: 160

P
pattern *(bottom)* layer: 11, 19, 24, 25, 29, 41, 73, 88, 110, 113, 134, 138, 141, 142, 148, 163
pick: 9
pick-up method: 148, 149, 151, 152
plain weave: 9, 113, 121, 123, 157, 158, 160
placemats: 22, 29, 31–33, 47, 49–51, 65–67, 69–71, 73, 75, 79–81, 83–85, 91, 103, 113, 115, 127, 136–139
potholders: 140–143
profile draft: 24, 135, 137, 141, 142

R
reed: See *sleying.*
reversible fabrics: 9, 29, 31, 35, 39
ribs: 9, 15, 19, 22, 27, 32, 37, 49, 50, 80, 94, 118, 143, 155
rugs: 10, 12, 13, 19, 23, 29, 42–45, 47, 52–55, 75, 91, 109–111, 151
runners: 29, 35–37, 39–41, 47, 49–51, 57–59, 61–63, 69–71, 73, 75, 79–81, 83–85, 91, 97–101, 113, 115, 127, 146, 151

S
samplers: 73, 75–77, 113, 125–131
samples, making: 15, 19, 62, 89, 125, 137, 146
Scandinavian drafting styles: 164, 166
Secretary box: 160, 161
selvedges: 13, 20, 21, 23, 33, 59
sett, determining: See *warp sett and weft sett.*
shed:
  clearing: 11
  opening: 21, 94, 100, 113, 148, 168
shrinkage: 19, 23, 32, 67, 71
shuttles:
  use of: 11, 15
  rotation of: 20, 21, 33, 37, 41, 45, 59, 63, 67, 77
skeleton tie-up: 21, 91, 94, 100, 101, 106, 111, 168
sleying: 20, 44, 88, 110, 137, 138, 141
solid lines: 24, 25, 47, 57, 58, 61, 63, 97, 139, 165
Solitaire Board: 147
squares, elongating: 15, 19, 22, 37, 89, 135, 143
Swedish double-thread method: See *double-thread method.*
sword: 11, 148

T
tabby weave, 20
table mats: 12, 29, 31–33, 87–89
take-up, warp: 19, 32, 137
Tapu'at (Mother and Child) maze: 152, 153
threading:
  draft: 25, 27, 73, 135, 138, 142
  heddles: 20, 25, 88, 110, 138
  key: 25, 52, 55, 73, 81, 84, 91, 105, 135, 138, 142
  reverse: 25, 73, 76, 113, 138, 142, 165
  styles: 163–168
  traditional method of: 167
Tic-Tac-Toe Game Board: 148
tie-down *(or binding)* thread: 9, 11, 15, 23

tie-up: 20, 21, 26, 40, 45, 100, 106, 139, 142, 167 (See also *skeleton tie-up.*)
top layer: See *background (top) layer.*
Traditional Checkerboard: 19, 146
treadles: 11, 20–21, 26, 167, 168
treadling:
  draft *(treadling sequence):* 26, 27, 135, 139, 143
  reverse: 26, 40, 126, 127
twill block: 91, 103, 105

W
wall hangings: 12, 13, 23, 75–77, 91, 103–105, 113, 115–119, 152
warp:
  chains: 44, 88, 110, 153
  length, determining: 19, 137, 141
  making the: 19, 25, 73, 88, 89, 110, 138
  materials: 11, 12, 13, 19
  sett: 12, 13, 15, 135, 136,
  winding the: 17, 20, 25
warp color sequence *(color key):* 20, 25, 83, 135, 138, 141
washing: 15, 19, 22, 23, 54, 94
weft:
  making: 15
  materials: 13, 15, 66
  nontraditional: 66
  sett: 15, 19, 22
  thickness: 9, 12, 13, 15, 19, 29, 37, 45, 89, 146
wefts, heavy and fine in same shed: 21, 33, 41, 59, 63, 77, 139
wide blocks, threading draft for: 164
Windmill Game Board: 149
windowpane pattern: 29, 35–37, 47, 49–51
wool: 11, 12, 23
working end: 12, 73, 88, 89, 109, 110

Y
yarn:
  sources: 169
  weights: 12, 13, 15, 52,
yarns, choosing: 12–13, 15, 135